Mindset Mentors

MINDSET MENTORS

240 of the Best Mentors Ever and Their Most Motivational Quotes

R.W. ROTH

CONTENTS

Part II. Film and TV

Part III. Music

Part IV. Business

Part V. Leaders

Part VI. Writers

Part VII. Philosophy

INTRODUCTION

This fact I know from personal experience: mindset is the single most important key to succeeding in life. With a healthy, positive mindset anything is possible. Without it, no number of external factors can help you. With this fact in mind it is important to note that anyone who has achieved anything notable has done so with the help of mentors imparting their wisdom on how to cultivate the correct mindset to succeed.

Mindset Mentors is about helping you achieve that mindset through the wisdom, inspiration and motivation of some of the most successful people on the planet — past, present, and from all walks of life. They range from sports superstars through to the wisest philosophers the world has ever known. It's the book I wish I'd had while growing up to help overcome the challenges life threw at me.

I failed pretty much all of my subjects in high school. I dropped out to become a boatbuilder, a job I thought I would enjoy but boy was I wrong. The hard, physical work, toxic environment and long days made getting blackout drunk on the weekends seem like paradise until hangovers and comedowns hit. Then it was straight back into another gruelling week of backbreaking work. Rinse and repeat this process for a few years and depression started to kick in.

Depressed, with an unhealthy mindset and contemplating whether it was worthwhile to carry on living, I came to the conclusion that I needed to change. I was searching for a mentor and someone to look up to when I came across Joe Rogan's podcast. His message — that challenging activities were essential to self-development and creating a calmer more balanced life — inspired me to start Brazilian Jiu Jitsu and a few years later, yoga.

This started to move my life in the right direction and slowly helped eliminate self-destructive habits. But I still needed to change my career path as that was a huge source of my unhappiness. Motivated by podcast episodes with successful guests such as Jordan Peterson and Gary Vaynerchuk, I started to read books on self-development and business.

Fast-forward a year and I believed that I had created the right mindset to enter into the entrepreneurial world. I jumped headfirst into starting a business with an acquaintance. It turns out we both knew nothing, money was lost, lessons were learnt, and I was back at square one which meant a lot more reading was required.

I let some time pass, just focusing on saving money, martial arts training and reading, which resulted in being offered an opportunity to help teach at the gym where I was training. This helped with some income and gave me the confidence to give business another shot, this time on my own. That previous experience helped my new venture to achieve success and has created a perfect, sustainable lifestyle balance.

It was a slow process to break the chains of depression and substance abuse. I achieved it by choosing to set my life's compass to constantly point towards becoming a better version of myself. This would have been impossible if I had not found mentors to look up to and borrow knowledge, ideas and habits from, to form my own healthy, positive mindset. And that's where the idea for this book came from, to share the thoughts that I have found most useful.

I have always loved quotes because they are often the only information that I can recall after reading a book. They stick in my mind while the rest of the writing goes straight to the subconscious. Sometimes they are almost like riddles that force me to think and figure out what is meant by that particular quote.

One powerful quote that affected me from the time I read it at age ten was from Friedrich Nietzsche: 'That which does not kill us makes us stronger'. To make sure it stuck with me, I had it tattooed in big lettering on my ribs so it would come to mind whenever I was confronted with the fear of failure and a decision had to be made.

I managed to pull myself out of some dark times by finding positive role models to follow and listen to and it is important to realise we all have a choice when deciding who and what we give our attention to in this digital age. What you focus on literally shapes how your life will turn out.

With a wide range of role models and mentors that share invaluable knowledge through their quotes, there is something here for everyone. Perhaps you are looking for some inspiration to add to your current mindset; or maybe you don't have any role models or mentors and are looking for advice on how to handle life's complexities. I hope this book will offer you the same value that I've received from the wisdom and encouragement of great mentors.

PART I

SPORT

@AYRTON SENNA

Formula One racer winning three championships

I have no idols. I admire work, dedication and competence.

Women — always in trouble with them, but can't live without them.

Money is a strange business. People who haven't got it aim for it strongly. People who have are full of troubles.

Wealthy men can't live on an island that is encircled by poverty. We all breathe the same air. We must give a chance to everyone, at least a basic chance.

I don't know driving in another way which isn't risky. Everyone has to improve themself. Each driver has their own limit. My limit is a little bit further than others.

These things bring you to reality as to how fragile you are; at the same moment you are doing something that nobody else is able to do. The same moment that you are seen as the best, the fastest and somebody that cannot be touched, you are enormously fragile.

And so you touch this limit, something happens and you suddenly can go a little bit further. With your mind power, your determination, your instinct, and the experience as well, you can fly very high.

Suddenly I realised that I was no longer driving the car consciously. I was driving it by a kind of instinct, only I was in a different dimension.

I continuously go further and further learning about my own limitations, my body limitations, psychological limitations. It's a way of life for me.

Because in a split second, it's gone.

Fear is exciting for me.

@BILLIE JEAN KING

Professional tennis player winning 12 Grand Slam singles titles

Champions keep playing until they get it right.

No one changes the world who isn't obsessed.

Pressure is a privilege — it only comes to those who earn it.

I think self-awareness is probably the most important thing towards being a champion.

Don't go into debt, and don't spend a lot. It's not how much money you make, it's how much you spend.

I love to promote our sport. I love grass-roots tennis. I love coaching. I love all parts of the sport. I love the business side.

It's just really important that we start celebrating our differences. Let's start tolerating first, but then we need to celebrate our differences.

I have often been asked whether I am a woman or an athlete. The question is absurd. Men are not asked that. I am an athlete. I am a woman.

Tennis taught me so many lessons in life. One of the things it taught me is that every ball that comes to me I have to make a decision. I have to accept responsibility for the consequences every time I hit a ball.

Sports teaches you character, it teaches you to play by the rules, it teaches you to know what it feels like to win and lose — it teaches you about life.

Face your fears; live your passions, be dedicated to your truth.

Don't let anyone define you. You define yourself.

Sports are a microcosm of society.

[3]

@CONOR MCGREGOR

First MMA fighter in the UFC to have been a champion in two divisions simultaneously

Life is about growing and improving and getting better.

To do anything at a high level, it has to be total obsession.

Why go through life if you're not going to challenge yourself?

I was always a dreamer, and my first ambition was to be a footballer.

Yes, sir, no, sir, clock in, clock out. Why were you late? Why are you not in today? That's not how humans are supposed to live.

I'm not going to get somewhere and say, 'OK, I'm done.' Success is never final; I'll just keep on going. The same way as failure never being fatal. Just keep going. I'm going to the stars and then past them.

I believe in believing. My coach John Kavanagh is a big atheist, and he is always trying to persuade people to his way of thinking, and I think, 'What a waste of energy.' If people want to believe in this god or that god, that's fine by me; believe away. But I think we can be our own gods. I believe in myself.

Doubt is only removed by action. If you're not working then that's when the doubt comes in.

Be grateful with everything you have and you will be successful in everything you do.

What someone else does or doesn't do has no effect on me and what I do.

I believe in myself so much that nothing is going to stop me.

All that matters is how you see yourself.

@CRISTIANO RONALDO

Professional soccer player

I will not quit.

Your love makes me strong. Your hate makes me unstoppable.

Dreams are not what you see in your sleep, dreams are things which do not let you sleep.

We cannot live being obsessed with what other people think about us. It's impossible to live like that. Not even God managed to please the entire world.

There is no harm in dreaming of becoming the world's best player. It is all about trying to be the best. I will keep working hard to achieve that, as it is within my capabilities.

There's no point in making predictions. It's not worth speculating because nothing is set in stone and things change all the time in football. Today there are opportunities that no one knows if they will come round again in the future.

Don't let small obstacles be in the way of being victorious. Remember you are stronger than the challenges you face.

When you have talent and if you don't work the talent then you are not going to win anything.

If you think you're perfect already, then you never will be.

If we can't help our family, who are we going to help?

@DAVID BECKHAM

Professional soccer player and businessman

The secret to my success is practice.

Being hardworking is the best thing you can show children.

You will go through tough times, it's about getting through them.

That was my way of getting through difficult times of low confidence — hard work.

Like any parent, I just want the best for my kids, whatever they decide to do. They will choose what path they want to follow, and we will always be there to encourage them.

I'm a very stubborn person. I think it has helped me over my career. I'm sure it has hindered me at times as well, but not too many times. I know that if I set my mind to do something, even if people are saying I can't do it, I will achieve it.

I respect all religions, but I'm not a deeply religious person. But I try to live life in the right way, respecting other people. I wasn't brought up in a religious way, but I believe there's something out there that looks after you.

It's so important to have manners and treat people from all walks of life the way they should be treated.

You can be the one in a million. Don't be discouraged by the odds to succeed.

The only time you run out of chances is when you stop taking them.

I still look at myself and want to improve.

Hindsight is a wonderful thing.

@ISRAEL ADESANYA

MMA fighter and UFC Middleweight champion

Insert inspirational/witty quote

It ain't about how you start it's about how you finish.

Some things money can't buy. Like actual friends, integrity or real skills.

If they knew I played with imaginary paddle shifts they'd have said I was crazy.

I draw a lot of inspiration from cartoon characters because they're more real than most people.

If you want to beat me, you should have done it yesterday because every single day I'm getting better.

Gratitude is my attitude. I used to sit by the water cooler during lunch at my old job and daydream of doing things like this. I wanna say something inspirational like an Insta-star, but straight up just look at my life, look at my story!! Enough said.

I been saying though. I'm responsible for what I say, I'm not responsible for how you interpret it.

No PR team needed. I don't do it for the likes. I do it for the love.

I just speak facts, no shade. But if the shoe fits, lace 'em up.

When I'm having fun, I'm the best in the world.

They can talk for you, they can't fight for you.

Not all heroes wear capes.

@JOHN WOODEN

Head coach for UCLA winning 10 NCAA national championships

Make each day your masterpiece.

Today is the only day. Yesterday is gone.

Discipline yourself, and others won't need to.

Do not let what you cannot do interfere with what you can do.

It's the little details that are vital. Little things make big things happen.

Things turn out best for the people who make the best of the way things turn out.

If you're not making mistakes, then you're not doing anything. I'm positive that a doer makes mistakes.

Be more concerned with your character than with your reputation. Your character is what you really are while your reputation is merely what others think you are.

Success is peace of mind which is a direct result of self-satisfaction in knowing you did your best to become the best you are capable of becoming.

Well, your greatest joy definitely comes from doing something for another, especially when it was done with no thought of something in return.

If you don't have time to do it right, when will you have time to do it over?

Failure is never fatal. But failure to change can and might be.

It's what you learn after you know it all that counts.

Never mistake activity for achievement.

It isn't what you do, but how you do it.

@KELLY SLATER

Professional surfer and winner of 11 world surfing championships

It's all about where your mind's at.

Motivation is temporary. Inspiration is permanent.

For a surfer, it's never-ending. There's always some wave you want to surf.

I want to surf better tomorrow. I want to surf better in 10 years. When I'm 50 I want to be a better surfer than I am now — for me it's a lifelong journey.

Not to sound too deep or weird, but I think that the times when you really appreciate surfing are the times you're really sort of becoming one with nature. Surfing's as raw of a sport as it gets.

Well I'm always working constantly on everything. I never take the approach that I'm doing as well as I possibly can, I always think there's more and I think if you don't have that, you are not driven to be better.

I've been in a poor physical shape many times in my career and I've had some of my best results. My best performances happened because my mind was in the right place. The mind is definitely stronger than the body.

I was just living in the moment. That's something I've been trying to do this year. I wasn't worried about anything that I couldn't control.

The joy of surfing is so many things combined, from the physical exertion of it, to the challenge of it, to the mental side of the sport.

Almost anything I've ever set my mind to, I could accomplish.

I've always thought surfing is a reflection of who you are.

Surfing is my religion, if I have one.

@KOBE BRYANT

Basketball player winning five championships in the NBA

If you're afraid to fail, then you're probably going to fail.

I don't want to be the next Michael Jordan, I only want to be Kobe Bryant.

Everything negative — pressure, challenges — is all an opportunity for me to rise.

It's the one thing you can control. You are responsible for how people remember you — or don't. So don't take it lightly.

If you want to be great at something, there's a choice you have to make. What I mean by that is, there are inherent sacrifices that come along with that. Family time, hanging out with friends, being a great friend, being a great son, nephew, whatever the case may be.

Pain doesn't tell you when you ought to stop. Pain is the little voice in your head that tries to hold you back because it knows if you continue you will change.

I can't relate to lazy people. We don't speak the same language. I don't understand you. I don't want to understand you.

The most important thing is to try and inspire people so that they can be great in whatever they want to do.

Haters are a good problem to have. Nobody hates the good ones. They hate the great ones.

I'm reflective only in the sense that I learn to move forward. I reflect with a purpose.

The moment you give up, is the moment you let someone else win.

@LEBRON JAMES

Basketball player winning three championships in the NBA

Nothing is given. Everything is earned.

Dream as if you'll live forever, live as if you'll die today.

Success isn't owned, it's leased. And the rent is due every day.

My dream has become a reality, and it's the best feeling I've ever had.

I think the reason why I am who I am today is because I went through those tough times when I was younger.

I don't need too much. Glamour and all that stuff don't excite me. I'm just glad I have the game of basketball in my life.

All your life you are told the things you cannot do. All your life they will say you're not good enough or strong enough or talented enough. They will say you're the wrong height or the wrong weight or the wrong type to play this or be this or achieve this. They will tell you no. A thousand times no. Until all the no's become meaningless. All your life they will tell you no. Quite firmly and very quickly. And you will tell them yes.

Warren Buffet told me once and he said, 'always follow your gut'. When you have that gut feeling, you have to go with, don't go back on it.

Greatness is defined by how much you want to put into what you do.

Hard work beats talent when talent fails to work hard.

Don't be afraid of failure. This is the way to succeed.

If I'm not giving 100 percent, I criticize myself.

I like criticism. It makes you strong.

@LIONEL MESSI

Professional soccer player

I do it because I love it and that's all I care about.

Sometimes you have to accept you can't win all the time.

The best decisions aren't made with your mind, but with your instinct.

I never think about the play or visualize anything. I do what comes to me at the moment. Instinct. It has always been that way.

Money is not a motivating factor. Money doesn't thrill me or make me play better because there are benefits to being wealthy. I'm just happy with a ball at my feet. My motivation comes from playing the game I love. If I wasn't paid to be a professional footballer I would willingly play for nothing.

This is why I didn't go out to parties and many other things. I am successful because I made sacrifices for success.

You have to fight to reach your dream. You have to sacrifice and work hard for it.

The day you think there are no improvements to be made is a sad day.

It took me 17 years and 114 days to become an overnight success.

I start early, and I stay late, day after day after day.

My ambition is always to get better and better.

@LOU HOLTZ

American football player, coach and analyst

Don't be a spectator, don't let life pass you by.

When all is said and done, more is said than done.

I never learn anything talking. I only learn things when I ask questions.

Life is ten percent what happens to you and ninety percent how you respond to it.

I follow three rules: Do the right thing, do the best you can, and always show people you care.

Don't tell your problems to people: eighty percent don't care; and the other twenty percent are glad you have them.

Successful people will always tell you that you can do something. It's the people who have never accomplished anything who will always discourage you from trying to achieve excellent things.

Ability is what you're capable of doing. Motivation determines what you do. Attitude determines how well you do it.

Show me someone who has done something worthwhile, and I'll show you someone who has overcome adversity.

The man who complains about the way the ball bounces is likely the one who dropped it.

If you burn your neighbors house down, it doesn't make your house look any better.

You'll never get ahead of anyone as long as you try to get even with them.

If what you did yesterday seems big, you haven't done anything today.

It's not the load that breaks you down, it's the way you carry it.

@MANNY PACQUIAO

Multiple time boxing world champion and Senator of the Philippines

All those who are around me are the bridge to my success, so they are all important.

I have to give people time to take a picture, and sign autographs. I have to be generous to people. It is in my heart. Without that, I would not be Manny Pacquiao.

I remember as a little boy I ate one meal a day and sometimes slept in the street. I will never forget that and it inspires me to fight hard, stay strong and remember all the people of my country trying to achieve better for themselves.

Anyone will succeed in whatever field of endeavor in life by acquiring the same virtues and character that boxing world champions do — dedication, perseverance, courage, extreme self-discipline and prayers.

Fearless is getting back up and fighting for what you want over and over again, even though every time you've tried before you've lost.

Sometimes I don't feel good, but when you get in the ring, you can't say "oh, I feel bad, can we stop?"

Success is sweet and sweeter if long delayed and gotten through many struggles and defeats.

I'm always having fun in training and in boxing. I think it's because boxing is my passion.

Life is meant to be a challenge because challenges are what make you grow.

Don't make training easy. Make it harder so that you will get better.

@MICHAEL JORDAN

Basketball player winning six championships in the NBA

You must expect great things of yourself before you can do them.

Never say never, because limits, like fears, are often just an illusion.

I can accept failure, everyone fails at something. But I can't accept not trying.

If it turns out that my best wasn't good enough, at least I won't look back and say I was afraid to try.

It is easy to choose a path of anonymity and lead an empty life. But to strive hard and lead an impactful life, one needs a burning desire to realize dreams.

Champions do not become champions when they win an event, but in the hours, weeks, and months, and years they spend preparing for it. The victorious performance itself is merely a demonstration of their championship character.

I've missed more than 9000 shots in my career. I've lost almost 300 games. 26 times, I've been trusted to take the game winning shot and missed. I've failed over and over and over again in my life. And that is why I succeed.

Obstacles don't have to stop you. If you run into a wall, don't turn around and give up. Figure out how to climb it, go through it, or work around it.

If you accept the expectations of others, especially negative ones, then you never will change the outcome.

Some people want it to happen, some wish it would happen, others make it happen.

If you do the work you get rewarded. There are no shortcuts in life.

Always turn a negative situation into a positive situation.

Learning's a gift, even when pain is your teacher.

@MICHAEL PHELPS

Record holding Olympic swimmer

If you say 'Can I?' You're restricting what you can do, or ever will do.

You can't put a limit on anything. The more you dream, the farther you get.

If you want to be the best, you have to do things that other people aren't willing to do.

The one thing that's common to all successful people. They make a habit of doing things that unsuccessful people don't like to do.

I think that everything is possible as long as you put your mind to it and you put the work and time into it. I think your mind really controls everything.

I like to just think of myself as a normal person who just has a passion, has a goal and a dream and goes out and does it. And that's really how I've always lived my life.

I think goals should never be easy, they should force you to work, even if they are uncomfortable at the time.

Things won't go perfect. It's all about how you adapt from those things and learn from mistakes.

There are always going to be obstacles that come in your way, stay positive.

I found something I love, and I never gave up.

@MUHAMMAD ALI

Heavyweight boxing champion regarded as one of the greatest boxers of all time

Silence is golden when you can't think of a good answer.

My principles are more important than the money or my title.

Service to others is the rent you pay for your room here on earth.

He who is not courageous enough to take risks will accomplish nothing in life.

If they can make penicillin out of mouldy bread, they can sure make something out of you.

A man who views the world the same at fifty as he did at twenty has wasted thirty years of his life.

I've made my share of mistakes along the way, but if I have changed even one life for the better, I haven't lived in vain.

I am an ordinary man who worked hard to develop the talent I was given. I believed in myself, and I believe in the goodness of others.

Rivers, ponds, lakes and streams — they all have different names, but they all contain water. Just as religions do — they all contain truths.

To be able to give away riches is mandatory if you wish to possess them. This is the only way that you will be truly rich.

It's the repetition of affirmations that leads to belief. And once that belief becomes a deep conviction, things begin to happen.

I hated every minute of training, but I said, 'Don't quit. Suffer now and live the rest of your life as a champion.'

It isn't the mountains ahead to climb that wear you out; it's the pebble in your shoe.

Don't count the days, make the days count.

@RICKSON GRACIE

Brazilian Jiu-Jitsu red belt regarded as one of the greatest MMA fighters of all time

Our fears don't stop death, they stop life.

Look around and find something for which to be grateful.

If today you have nothing to be happy about, thank God for the potential of tomorrow.

I always keep my mind open. For me, a mind has to work like a parachute, it works only if it's open.

Everybody has fear. The difference is that the coward does not control fear and the brave gets over it.

I believe intelligence and fear are very close together. Guys who say they are not afraid of anything, they are stupid. They are silly to me. I am afraid of everything.

If you do not speak up when it matters, when would it matter that you speak? The opposite of courage is conformity. Even a dead fish can go with the flow.

Jiu-jitsu puts you completely in the moment, where you must have a complete focus on finding a solution to the problem. This trains the mind to build that focus, to increase your awareness, your capacity to solve problems.

Physical strength (hard work), mental strength (perseverance) and spiritual strength (love & acceptance) are the keys to continuous growth.

The biggest gift I received as a martial artist is without a question the capacity to be in peace.

Sometimes, you don't have to win, you cannot win. But that has nothing to do with losing.

If size mattered, the elephant would be king of the jungle.

Willingness to learn is the mark of a youthful mind.

@ROGER FEDERER

Professional tennis player winning 20 Grand Slam singles titles

I always look at the long term.

There's no way around hard work. Embrace it.

You have to put in the hours because there's always something which you can improve.

I always believe if you're stuck in a hole and maybe things aren't going well you will come out stronger. Everything in life is this way.

It is always in my mind still that I can crush anybody. That's not an issue. But I think that is the same for most athletes. If you don't believe you can win tournaments anymore, then you can't do it.

Success is a nice thing because it always means you've taken a step forward and it gives you a sense of pride, which in turn gives you confidence and experience, a positive circle, so to speak.

One of my big, big strengths I think early on in my career was that I could learn very quickly. You wouldn't have to tell me the things 10 times or 50 times until I would understand them. You would only have to tell me two or three times.

You have to put in a lot of sacrifice and effort for sometimes little reward but you have to know that if you put in the right effort the reward will come.

Once you find that peace, that place of peace and quiet, harmony and confidence, that's when you start playing your best.

You have to believe in the long-term plan you have but you need the short-term goals to motivate and inspire you.

When you're good at something, make that everything.

I fear no one but respect everyone.

@RONDA ROUSEY

Olympic Judoka, MMA fighter and the first UFC champion in the female bantamweight division

I'm scared of failure all the time, but I'm not scared enough to stop trying.

I go to bed every night thinking about all the possible ways that I can succeed.

The knowledge that everything good can be taken away at any second is what makes me work so hard.

People say to me all the time, 'You have no fear.' I tell them, 'No, that's not true. I'm scared all the time. You have to have fear in order to have courage. I'm a courageous person because I'm a scared person.

When I was in school, martial arts made you a dork, and I became self-conscious that I was too masculine. I was a 16-year-old girl with ringworm and cauliflower ears. People made fun of my arms and called me 'Miss Man.' It wasn't until I got older that I realized: These people are idiots. I'm fabulous.

My first injury ever was a broken toe, and my mother made me run laps around the mat for the rest of the night. She said she wanted me to know that even if I was hurt, I was still fine.

No one is ever going to give you anything of value. You have to work for it, sweat for it, fight for it. But there is far greater value in accomplishments you earn than in accolades that are merely given to you. When you earn something, you never have to worry about justifying that you truly deserve it.

Everyone wants to win. But to truly succeed — whether it is at a sport or at your job or in life — you have to be willing to do the hard work, overcome the challenges, and make the sacrifices it takes to be the best at what you do.

Life is a fight from the minute you take your first breath to the moment you exhale your last. Even if they don't know it, everyone has the instinct to survive.

Fighting is not a man's thing, it is a human thing.

@RYAN SHECKLER

Professional skateboarder and entrepreneur

I'm going to capitalize on everything I can.

I won the first contest I ever entered, when I was 6.

My whole life has been the skate life. I don't really remember doing anything besides skateboarding.

If you go out there and your main purpose is to get a sponsor, then it's not gonna work. Just go out there and have fun. That's how I got sponsored.

Whatever sport you choose, do it because you love it, and don't expect to be an expert first thing. It takes time to do well at anything, but if you love it, you'll stick with it.

I run a lot. I do a lot of yoga. Hot yoga. Which is random and sounds lame, but it has definitely made my flexibility and balance 100 percent better on my skateboard. I do that and a lot of plyometrics, biometrics, and surfing. I train every other day of the week and skate for an hour everyday.

I like skateboarding. I'm here on this planet to skateboard; I feel this is what God wants me to do. I just live it. I get hurt all the time. I break bones. It's just all part of the process.

I'm living with every step. I can't live with regret. The past is the past. I'm not worried about it. I can't change it. I can't fix it. It is what it is. I'm just living.

Don't ever give up. You gotta keep trying, and never give up.

I just want to keep things going. I just love testing myself.

@SERENA WILLIAMS

Professional tennis player winning 23 Grand Slam singles titles

I'm definitely not a fearless individual.

You have to believe in yourself when no one else does.

Am I the greatest? I don't know. I'm the greatest that I can be.

I am lucky that whatever fear I have inside me, my desire to win is always stronger.

I don't like to lose — at anything, yet I've grown most not from victories, but setbacks. If winning is God's reward, then losing is how he teaches us.

With a defeat, when you lose, you get up, you make it better, you try again. That's what I do in life, when I get down, when I get sick, I don't want to just stop. I keep going and I try to do more. Everyone always says never give up but you really have to take that to heart and really never give up. Keep trying.

Luck has nothing to do with it, because I have spent many, many hours, countless hours, on the court working for my one moment in time, not knowing when it would come.

I always believe I can beat the best, achieve the best. I always see myself in the top position.

Everything comes at a cost. Just what are you willing to pay for it?

I think in life you should work on yourself until the day you die.

If Plan A isn't working, I have Plan B, Plan C, and even Plan D.

Don't let anybody work harder than you do.

@TRAVIS PASTRANA

Motorsports competitor winning multiple X-Games championships

In life, you're along for the ride either way. You might as well make it fun!

Somewhere in the fear and chaos, there is a clarity that few will ever experience.

Other people don't know what you've gone through. And everybody has a story that you probably don't know.

I really enjoy being home because that's where family is. No matter where you're from, it's hard to beat home.

Everyone that works behind a desk wants to know how many bones I've broken and how much money I make. It seems that people who've never experienced the excitement of sport seem to think the only thing worth taking risks for is money.

Nothing's about taking risks as much as doing stuff that other people haven't done before. Just like in racing, it's not about taking risks but trying to figure out how to be faster.

I'm just competitive. Everybody always says, 'You've gotta be crazy to do what you do.' It's not really true. Everything we do is always about trying to out-do your friends. Trying to one-up, be a little faster, a little better, jump a little further.

My strengths and weaknesses are the same: I've got the willingness and stupidity to try anything. If I think it's even remotely possible, I'll do it.

There's no such thing as boundaries, only limits that get pushed further and further.

Every day I push myself to redefine the limits of our sport.

@TYSON FURY

Two-time heavyweight boxing world champion

Exterior assets mean nothing if you can't control what's going on inside.

Mental health has got to be the biggest battle I've ever fought with, more than any opponent.

If I can show the world that you can come back from it (depression), and get back in shape and to the top, then anybody can do it.

It won't be a great day every day. I used to wake up and think, why did I not die in my sleep last night. But there will be rose-colored sunshine days again. Maybe not today or tomorrow, but seek medical advice and it will get better, I promise you this.

People really don't understand about mental health problems unless you've been through it. Looking from the outside in, people say well, that's an idiot. He's got everything going for him and he's still not happy. If I knew what it was, then I'd have fixed it straight away.

Foolish people follow the system, get caught up in media news, what the government wants you to believe and all the higher powers want you to believe and go down the same path as all the sheep in the cattle market.

Whatever is conventional, I am the opposite. So if you want to walk in a straight line, I am going to walk in zig zags. If you want to throw a 1-2, I'll throw a 2-1.

All I care about is providing and living every day. I don't care about world titles, being a legend, or being a hero.

The past is the past. What happened yesterday is history. I look forward to the future on a daily basis.

@USAIN BOLT

Record holding Olympic sprinter

Win from within.

Learning about the mind is as important as understanding the body.

The difference between the impossible and the possible lies in determination.

I know what I can do so it doesn't bother me what other people think or their opinion on the situation.

For me, I'm focused on what I want to do. I know what I need to do to be a champion, so I'm working on it.

Dreams are free. Goals have a cost. While you can daydream for free, goals don't come without a price. Time, effort, sacrifice, and sweat. How will you pay for your goals?

When I was younger, I always wanted to impress, to be good for my country, to make them feel good, and sometimes that meant I didn't focus on myself enough. I learned I had to put myself first. And it's fine because I want for myself the same thing that they want for me, which is to win.

Manners is the key thing. Say, for instance, when you're growing up, you're walking down the street, you've got to tell everybody good morning. Everybody. You can't pass one person.

Worrying gets you nowhere. If you turn up worrying about how you're going to perform, you've already lost. Train hard, turn up, run your best and the rest will take care of itself.

I know what to do and I go and execute.

@VINCE LOMBARDI

American football coach

Once you learn to quit, it becomes a habit.

Winning is not everything, but wanting to win is.

God, family and the Green Bay Packers, in that order.

The only place success comes before work is in the dictionary.

Perfection is not attainable, but if we chase perfection we can catch excellence.

Excellence must be pursued, it must be wooed with all of one's might and every bit of effort that we have each day there's a new encounter, each week is a new challenge.

The price of success is hard work, dedication to the job at hand, and the determination that whether we win or lose, we have applied the best of ourselves to the task at hand.

It's easy to have faith in yourself and have discipline when you're a winner, when you're number one. What you have to have is faith and discipline when you're not a winner.

The difference between a successful person and others is not a lack of strength, not a lack of knowledge, but rather a lack of will.

Character is just another word for having a perfectly disciplined and educated will.

It's not whether you get knocked down, it's whether you get up.

Winning is a habit. Unfortunately, so is losing.

Fatigue makes cowards of us all.

PART II

FILM AND TV

@ANGELINA JOLIE

Award winning actress, filmmaker and humanitarian

People say that you're going the wrong way when it's simply a way of your own.

If you ask people what they've always wanted to do, most people haven't done it. That breaks my heart.

Our diversity is our strength. What a dull and pointless life it would be if everyone was the same.

If every choice you make comes from an honest place, you're solid, and nothing anybody can say about you can rock you or change your opinion.

Without pain, there would be no suffering, without suffering we would never learn from our mistakes. To make it right, pain and suffering is the key to all windows, without it, there is no way of life.

There's something about death that is comforting. The thought that you could die tomorrow frees you to appreciate your life now.

If you don't get out of the box you've been raised in, you won't understand how much bigger the world is.

Make bold choices and make mistakes. It's all those things that add up to the person you become.

If I make a fool of myself, who cares? I'm not frightened by anyone's perception of me.

I will do the best I can with this life, to be of use.

@ARNOLD SCHWARZENEGGER

Actor, businessman, former politician and professional bodybuilder

The more knowledge you have, the more you're free to rely on your instincts.

What is the point of being on this Earth if you are going to be like everyone else?

For me life is continuously being hungry. The meaning of life is not simply to exist, to survive, but to move ahead, to go up, to achieve, to conquer.

The mind is the limit. As long as the mind can envision the fact that you can do something, you can do it, as long as you really believe 100 percent.

It's not what you get out of life that counts. Break your mirrors! In our society that is so self-absorbed, begin to look less at yourself and more at each other. You'll get more satisfaction from having improved your neighborhood, your town, your state, your country, and your fellow human beings than you'll ever get from your muscles, your figure, your automobile, your house, or your credit rating.

Help others and give something back. I guarantee you will discover that while public service improves the lives and the world around you, its greatest reward is the enrichment and new meaning it will bring your own life.

Positive thinking can be contagious. Being surrounded by winners helps you develop into a winner.

You have to remember something: Everybody pities the weak; jealousy you have to earn.

Strength does not come from winning. Your struggles develop your strengths.

@AUDREY HEPBURN

Actress and humanitarian

To plant a garden is to believe in tomorrow.

Giving is living. If you stop wanting to give, there's nothing more to live for.

Success is like reaching an important birthday and finding you're exactly the same.

I've been lucky. Opportunities don't often come along. So, when they do, you have to grab them.

Good things aren't supposed to just fall into your lap. God is very generous, but he expects you to do your part first.

As you grow older, you will discover that you have two hands, one for helping yourself, the other for helping others.

Not to live for the day, that would be materialistic — but to treasure the day. I realize that most of us live on the skin, on the surface, without appreciating just how wonderful it is simply to be alive at all.

Pick the day. Enjoy it — to the hilt. The day as it comes. People as they come, the past, I think, has helped me appreciate the present — and I don't want to spoil any of it by fretting about the future.

For beautiful eyes, look for the good in others; for beautiful lips, speak only words of kindness; and for poise, walk with the knowledge that you are never alone.

The most important thing is to enjoy your life, to be happy, it's all that matters.

Nothing is impossible, the word itself says 'I'm possible'!

@BRUCE LEE

Martial artist, actor and philosopher

Be happy, but never satisfied.

To hell with circumstances; I create opportunities.

The key to immortality is first living a life worth remembering.

Mistakes are always forgivable, if one has the courage to admit them.

If you spend too much time thinking about a thing, you'll never get it done.

For it is easy to criticize and break down the spirit of others, but to know yourself takes a lifetime.

I'm not in this world to live up to your expectations and you're not in this world to live up to mine.

To live is to express, and to express you have to create. Creation is never merely repetition. To live is to express oneself freely in creation.

Instead of buying your children all the things you never had, you should teach them all the things you were never taught. Material wears out but knowledge stays.

It is not how much you have learned, but how much you have absorbed in what you have learned.

Absorb what is useful, discard what is useless and add what is specifically your own.

The poorer we are inwardly, the more we try to enrich ourselves outwardly.

Do not pray for an easy life, pray for the strength to endure a difficult one.

If you love life, don't waste time, for time is what life is made up of.

The more we value things, the less we value ourselves.

Long-term consistency trumps short-term intensity.

@DANNY TREJO

Actor and entrepreneur

I think I'm a workaholic, but I'm a workaholic that is loving his work.

Everything good that's ever happened to me came out of helping others.

If you look at the people in Hollywood who are heavy partiers, they're selfish, self-centered and egotistical.

Acting is just a job. I'm exactly the same as that lady bringing us coffee, and I have to remember that.

The first five years of my career, I was Inmate #1, Bad Guy #1 and Mean Guy #1. I had a great career going, until somebody told me that I was typecast. I said, "Well, what's typecast?" And they said, "Well, you're always playing the mean Chicano dude with tattoos." I thought about that and I said, "Wait a minute! I am the mean Chicano dude with tattoos, so somebody is getting it right."

I didn't make a deal with God, because you can't make a deal with God. He put me here to talk to kids and to talk to drunks and help addicts. He gave me this "job" which makes it a lot easier to get through to people.

There is no significance of God in my life, God is my life. I would not be, without God. I am supposed to be dead.

When people come at me they can't win, they think they can, but they can't. I'll just walk away.

Nobody gets killed when they're happy. It always starts with an argument, or a debt.

Anybody over 40 is an older person. You better give them some respect.

I never imagined that I'd be out of prison.

@DAVE CHAPPELLE

Comedian and creator of Chappelle's Show

You have to be careful of the company you keep.

If you don't have the right people around you and you're moving at a million miles an hour, you can lose yourself.

One of the things that happen when people make the leap from a certain amount of money to tens of millions of dollars is that the people around you dramatically change.

Most of the people around me have a vested interest in how much money I make. You know, so a celebrity could find themselves in a position where people could have meetings about their life without them involved. And when I say 'their life' I mean not their professional life either. They could talk about their personal life.

I just always loved stand-up. It's like magic. You say something, and a whole room full of people laughs together. Say something else, they laugh again. The fact that people come to see that and participate in that, I don't know, it's just like magic.

You've got to say 'yes' to your destiny. Life's happening right now, look around you. There goes some life. Come on, Mamma, live!

The world can't tell you who you are. You've just got to figure out who you are and be there, for better or worse.

Money is the fuel for choices. Money gives me choices, so it's not nothing, it's something.

If I can make a teacher's salary doing comedy, I think that's better than being a teacher.

Constantly take inventory of what's important to you.

@DWAYNE 'THE ROCK' JOHNSON

Actor, producer and businessman

We are all a work in progress.

All success begins with self-discipline. It starts with you.

Be humble. Be hungry. And always be the hardest worker in the room.

Success isn't always about 'Greatness', it's about consistency. Consistent, hard work gains success. Greatness will come.

Check your ego at the door. The ego can be the great success inhibitor. It can kill opportunities, and it can kill success.

Show respect even to people who don't deserve it; not as a reflection of their character, but a reflection of yours.

I found that with depression, one of the most important things you could realise is that you're not alone.

Success isn't overnight. It's when everyday you get a little better than the day before. It all adds up.

Don't be afraid to be ambitious about your goals. Hard work never stops. Neither should your dreams.

In 1995 I had $7 in my pocket and I knew two things: I'm broke as hell and one day I won't be.

You have to fight through some bad days to earn the best days of your life.

Blood, sweat and respect. First two you give, last one you earn.

Let your actions do your talking for you.

@ELLEN DEGENERES

Comedian and host of The Ellen DeGeneres Show

Sometimes you can't see yourself clearly until you see yourself through the eyes of others.

True beauty is not related to what color your hair is or what color your eyes are. True beauty is about who you are as a human being, your principles, your moral compass.

Here are the values that I stand for: honesty, equality, kindness, compassion, treating people the way you want to be treated and helping those in need. To me, those are traditional values.

I am saddened by how people treat one another and how we are so shut off from one another and how we judge one another, when the truth is, we are all one connected thing. We are all from the same exact molecules.

Life is like one big Mardi Gras. But instead of showing boobs, show people your brain, and if they like what they see, you'll have more beads than you know what to do with.

I work really hard at trying to see the big picture and not getting stuck in ego. I believe we're all put on this planet for a purpose, and we all have a different purpose. When you connect with that love and that compassion, that's when everything unfolds.

It's our challenges and obstacles that give us layers of depth and make us interesting. Are they fun when they happen? No. But they are what make us unique. And that's what I know for sure, I think.

It is failure that gives you the proper perspective on success.

@GEORGE CLOONEY

Award winning actor, film producer and director

You can only get so far without discernible talent.

I rarely tell anybody what they should be doing with their life.

I find that as you get older, you start to simplify things in general.

You need to have flopped quite a few times to get a sense of how little any of it has to do with you.

I'm kind of comfortable with getting older because it's better than the other option, which is being dead. So I'll take getting older.

When you're young you believe it when people tell you how good you are. And that's the danger, you inhale. Everyone will tell you you're a genius, which you are not, and if you understand that, you win.

Art takes different forms, but it represents something that is basic in all of us—our history.

I don't like to share my personal life, it wouldn't be personal if I shared it.

You never really learn much from hearing yourself speak.

Failures are infinitely more instructive than successes.

The only failure is not to try.

@GEORGE LUCAS

Filmmaker best known for creating the Star Wars series

It's in the doing that you prove yourself.

The ability to speak does not make you intelligent.

Education is the single most important job of the human race.

One thing about Star Wars that I'm really proud of is that it expands the imagination.

The best way to pursue happiness is to help other people. Nothing else will make you happier.

You have to find something that you love enough to be able to take risks, jump over hurdles and break through the brick walls that are always going to be placed in front of you. If you don't have that kind of feeling for what it is you are doing, you'll stop at the first giant hurdle.

A lot of people like to do certain things, but they're not that good at it. Keep going through the things that you like to do until you find something that you actually seem to be extremely good at. It can be anything.

The secret is not to give up hope. It's very hard not to because if you're really doing something worthwhile I think you will be pushed to the brink of hopelessness before you come through the other side.

Working hard is very important. You're not going to get anywhere without working extremely hard.

Everybody has talent, it's just a matter of moving around until you've discovered what it is.

Dreams are extremely important. You can't do it unless you imagine it.

Always remember, your focus determines your reality.

We are all living in cages with the door wide open.

@JENNIFER ANISTON

Actress, film producer and business woman

There are no regrets in life, just lessons.

I always say don't make plans, make options.

When you try to avoid the pain, it creates greater pain.

It's impossible to satisfy everyone, and I suggest we all stop trying.

People who avoid the brick walls — all power to ya, but we all have to hit them sometimes in order to push through to the next level, to evolve.

I think it's always important to reflect anyway, no matter what age you're approaching or what milestone is in front of you. Reflection should be almost a daily thing if possible.

Beauty is inner confidence. Peace. Kindness. Honesty. A life well-lived. Taking on challenges and not feeling shame for things that haven't gone the way you felt they should have.

Once you figure out who you are and what you love about yourself, I think it all kinda falls into place.

Really try to follow what it is that you want to do and what your heart is telling you to do.

I don't have a religion. I believe in God. My own interpretation of the supernatural.

The greater your capacity to love, the greater your capacity to feel the pain.

What inspires you, what excites you when you wake up in the morning?

I realized it was only me who was stopping myself from living my life.

If you're not happy, you can become happy. Happiness is a choice.

@JIM CARREY

Award winning actor, comedian, producer and artist

I don't make it in regular channels, and that's okay for me.

Maybe other people will try to limit me but I don't limit myself.

Life opens up opportunities to you, and you either take them or you stay afraid of taking them.

If you aren't in the moment, you are either looking forward to uncertainty, or back to pain and regret.

I really believe in the philosophy that you create your own universe. I'm just trying to create a good one for myself.

As far as I can tell, it's just about letting the universe know what you want and then working toward it while letting go of how it comes to pass.

I wake up some mornings and sit and have my coffee and look out at my beautiful garden, and I go, 'Remember how good this is. Because you can lose it.'

I know this sounds strange, but as a kid, I was really shy. Painfully shy. The turning point was freshman year, when I was the biggest geek alive. No one, I mean no one, even talked to me.

Desperation is a necessary ingredient to learning anything, or creating anything. Period. If you ain't desperate at some point, you ain't interesting.

I think everybody should get rich and famous and do everything they ever dreamed of so they can see that it's not the answer.

It is better to risk starving to death than surrender. If you give up on your dreams, what's left?

@JOE ROGAN

Comedian, podcaster and UFC commentator

Martial arts are a vehicle for developing your human potential.

By putting yourself in that intense form of stress, it makes regular life more peaceful.

One of the most fascinating lessons I've absorbed about life is that the struggle is good.

There's a direct correlation between positive energy and positive results in the physical form.

As a longtime practitioner of yoga and a person who's been involved in physical fitness my whole life, I can tell you, yoga helps you achieve altered states of consciousness. It is not just stretching. The only way you can say that it's stretching is if you haven't done it, or that you haven't done it rigorously for a long period of time.

If you ever start taking things too seriously, just remember that we are talking monkeys on an organic spaceship flying through the universe.

The key to happiness doesn't lay in numbers in a bank account but in the way we make others feel and the way they make us feel.

Be cool to people. Be nice to as many people as you can. Smile to as many people as you can, and have them smile back at you.

The time you spend hating on someone robs you of your own time. You are literally hating on yourself and you don't even realize it.

Greatness and madness are next door neighbors and they often borrow each other's sugar.

Kindness is one of the best gifts you can bestow, we know inherently that it feels great.

Someone else's success does not equal a failure for you.

Be the hero of your own story.

@KEANU REEVES

Actor, producer and director

Tomorrow isn't guaranteed, so live today!

Mortality is very different when you're 20 to when you're 50.

When I don't feel free and can't do what I want, I just react. I go against it.

You have to change your life if you're not happy, and wake up if things aren't going the way you want.

The recognition of the law of cause and effect, also known as karma, is a fundamental key to understanding how you've created your world, with actions of your body, speech, and mind. When you truly understand karma, then you realize you are responsible for everything in your life. It is incredibly empowering to know that your future is in your hands.

Money doesn't mean anything to me. I've made a lot of money, but I want to enjoy life and not stress myself building my bank account. I give lots away and live simply, mostly out of a suitcase in hotels. We all know that good health is much more important.

Sure I believe in God and the Devil, but they don't have to have pitchforks and a long white beard.

I was raised to treat people exactly how I would like to be treated by others. It's called respect.

The person who was holding me back from my happiness was me.

Sometimes simple things are the most difficult things to achieve.

The simple act of paying attention can take you a long way.

Grief changes shape, but it never ends.

@KEVIN HART

Comedian, actor and producer

A reputation as a hard worker is a good reputation to have.

I don't care how busy I am — I will always make time for what's most important to me.

The day you stop doing the small things is the day you think you're above everybody else.

Life is too short to worry about what others say about you. Have fun and give them something to talk about.

Everybody wants to be famous, but nobody wants to do the work. I live by that. You grind hard so you can play hard. At the end of the day, you put all the work in, and eventually it'll pay off. It could be in a year, it could be in 30 years. Eventually your hard work will pay off.

Appreciate the hard work and the process of hard work. Because after that's over and you get the rewards of success, you look back on those moments and you respect those moments the best.

It all depends on what you're willing to invest time and effort in and put your mind to. That's what separates winners from losers. Winners are the ones who want the most out of their opportunities.

No matter what, people grow. If you choose not to grow, you're staying in a small box with a small mindset. People who win go outside of that box. It's very simple when you look at it.

If you give up at the first sign of struggle, you're really not ready to be successful.

The only time you should look back in life is to see how far you have come.

Everybody that's successful lays a blueprint out.

@LEONARDO DICAPRIO

Award winning actor and producer

To join the top 1% you have to do what the 99% won't.

Pay close attention to people who don't clap when you win.

If you want to be successful, respect one rule. Never let failure take control of you.

Only you and you alone can change your situation. Don't blame it on anything or anyone.

If you can do what you do best and be happy, you're further along in life than most people.

Money was always on my mind when I was growing up. So I was always wondering how we were going to afford this and that. Acting seemed to be a shortcut out of the mess.

I really hate relaxing. I've done three movies in a row, worked for two years straight, and to me, idle time is the devil's workshop. I like to focus on something.

Everybody has gone through something that has changed them in a way that they could never go back to the person they once were.

School, I never truly got the knack of. I could never focus on things I didn't want to learn.

We are all shaped from memories we have as young people.

Be thankful for the hard times, for they have made you.

@MERYL STREEP

Academy award winning actress

I think your true self emerges more clearly over time.

The minute you start caring about what other people think, is the minute you stop being yourself.

True freedom is understanding that we have a choice in who and what we allow to have power over us.

People will say to me, 'You've played so many strong women' and I'll say, 'Have you ever said to a man, 'You've played so many strong men?'

Power, influence, strength — all those things can overpower what's important in life. But as long as you have food and shelter over your head, if the necessities are taken care of, what makes us happy on top of that is very simple.

I think that you find your own way, in the end, it's what feels right to you. Not what your mother told you. Not what some actress told you. Not what anybody else told you but the still, small voice.

It's good to push yourself and do what you don't necessarily want to do, that if you're not automatically good at it, you should try it. Trying is so important.

The formula of happiness and success is just being yourself, in the most vivid possible way you can.

Put blinders onto those things that conspire to hold you back, especially the ones in your own head.

@MORGAN FREEMAN

Award winning actor and film narrator

The best way to guarantee a loss is to quit.

As long as you feel like a victim, you are one.

Challenge yourself; it's the only path which leads to growth.

Never let pride be your guiding principle. Let your accomplishments speak for you.

Learning how to be still, to really be still and let life happen — that stillness becomes a radiance.

Don't be different just for different's sake. If you see it differently, function that way. Follow your own muse, always.

Was I always going to be here? No I was not. I was going to be homeless at one time, a taxi driver, truck driver, or any kind of job that would get me a crust of bread. You never know what's going to happen.

Very often, you know, you stop walking because you say, 'Well, I'm tired of climbing this hill. I'm never going to get to the top.' And you're only two steps from the top.

If your life turns out to be good and you have a tremendous amount of luck in your life, it's a good thing to turn around and make it work for others.

I can say that life is good to me. Has been and is good. So I think my task is to be good to it. How do you be good to life? You live it.

I once heard a wise man say there are no perfect men. Only perfect intentions.

How do we change the world? One random act of kindness at a time.

If you want to see a miracle, be the miracle.

@OPRAH WINFREY

Talk show host, TV producer, philanthropist and author of The Path Made Clear

When you undervalue what you do, the world will undervalue who you are.

The more you praise and celebrate your life, the more there is in life to celebrate.

Be thankful for what you have; you'll end up having more. If you concentrate on what you don't have, you will never, ever have enough.

I don't think of myself as a poor deprived ghetto girl who made good. I think of myself as somebody who from an early age knew I was responsible for myself, and I had to make good.

What material success does is provide you with the ability to concentrate on other things that really matter. And that is being able to make a difference, not only in your own life, but in other people's lives.

Do the one thing you think you cannot do. Fail at it. Try again. Do better the second time. The only people who never tumble are those who never mount the high wire. This is your moment. Own it.

One of the hardest things in life to learn are which bridges to cross and which bridges to burn.

What I know is, if you do work that you love, and the work fulfills you, the rest will come.

Passion is energy. Feel the power that comes from focusing on what excites you.

I don't believe in failure. It is not failure if you enjoyed the process.

Turn your wounds into wisdom.

@ROBERT DE NIRO

Actor, producer and director

Talent is in the choices.

If you don't go, you'll never know.

You'll have time to rest when you're dead.

Feeling a little bit alive is a lot better than just waiting to die.

Time goes on. So whatever you're going to do, do it. Do it now. Don't wait.

When you are working hard, you don't have time for anything other than what you are doing.

A lot of young actors have the idea that, 'I've got to do this right. There's a right way to do this.' But there's no right or wrong. There's only good and bad. And 'bad' usually happens when you're trying too hard to do it right. There's a very broad spectrum of things that can inhibit you. The most important thing for actors — and not just actors, but everybody — is to feel loose enough to create what you want to create, and be free to try anything. To have choices.

Sometimes if you have financial restraints, it's a benefit. It forces you to come up with a more creative way.

There is only one way to gain access to the truth and that is to not expect anything.

Life rarely changes you totally but it consistently changes you in details.

Passion should always trump common sense.

The saddest thing in life is wasted talent.

@ROBERT DOWNEY JR.

Actor and producer

Worrying is like praying for something that you don't want to happen.

Do I want to be a hero to my son? No. I would like to be a very real human being. That's hard enough.

There are some parents who have really done it right and told their kid, you know, we have this dough, none of this is for you. You have to get your own.

All I want, and I think all any parent with a semblance of a moral psychology wants, is for my kid to have his own experience, uninhibited.

I used to be so convinced that happiness was the goal, yet all those years I was chasing after it I was unhappy in the pursuit. Maybe the goal really should be a life that values honor, duty, good work, friends, and family.

Mediocrity is my biggest fear. I'm not afraid of total failure because I don't think that will happen. I'm not afraid of success because that beats the hell out of failure. It's being in the middle that scares me.

People rise out of the ashes because, at some point, they are invested with a belief in the possibility of triumph over seemingly impossible odds.

Remember that just because you hit bottom doesn't mean you have to stay there.

Listen, smile, agree and then do whatever you were gonna do anyway.

Nothing will serve you better than a strong work ethic. Nothing.

@SIMON COWELL

TV personality and judge on multiple talent shows such as American Idol and X-Factor

Being different is good; embrace it.

Not everybody is perfect, and I don't think we should be looking for perfect people.

Praise a stranger with a few nice words and he becomes a stranger that calls you a friend.

When someone asks, 'Does success make you into a monster?' I always say, No, it enables you to be a monster.

I think of stress as the creator of cancer and heart attacks, like a tiny little ball you feed. I believe that one of the reasons I've never got ill is that I'm not stressed.

Every single negative can lead to a positive. With any negative situation don't get too down about it — you'll work it out. You learn it as you go along. You don't get smart at 17. You just don't unless you're one of a billion. It will happen over time and it's the getting there which will be the most fun.

My dad said to me, 'Work hard and be patient.' It was the best advice he ever gave me. You have to put the hours in.

You don't go into anything contemplating failure, because if you did, you wouldn't make it.

I got good advice once. Someone said to me: Live in your money rather than look at it.

What other people think about me is none of my business.

People confuse ego, lust and insecurity with true love.

@STEVE HARVEY

Comedian and host of multiple TV shows including Family Feud

What would you do if you weren't afraid?

The dream is free, but the hustle is sold separately.

4 P's to success: pressure, persistence, perseverance & prayer.

When you're happy at home, you can make a lot of things happen.

Your career is what you're paid for, your calling is what you're made for.

Do not ignore the passion that burns in you. Spend time to discover your gift.

If you want to be successful you have to jump, there's no way around it. If you're safe, you'll never soar.

Failure is a great teacher, and I think when you make mistakes and you recover from them and you treat them as valuable learning experiences, then you've got something to share.

You simply cannot drive forward if you are completely focused on what's happening in the rear view mirror.

The more people you help become successful the more successful you become.

Sometimes out of your biggest misery, comes your greatest gain.

Growth is in a series of mistakes. That's the only way you learn.

If you want to kill a big dream, tell it to a small-minded person.

You are never too old to reinvent yourself.

@STEVEN SPIELBERG

Film director, producer and screenwriter

All good ideas start out as bad ideas, that's why it takes so long.

I don't dream at night, I dream at day, I dream all day; I'm dreaming for a living.

Even though I get older, what I do never gets old, and that's what I think keeps me hungry.

I never felt comfortable with myself, because I was never part of the majority. I always felt awkward and shy and on the outside of the momentum of my friends' lives.

I've always been very hopeful which I guess isn't strange coming from me. I don't want to call myself an optimist. I want to say that I've always been full of hope. I've never lost that. I have a lot of hope for this country and for the entire world.

Sometimes a dream almost whispers, it never shouts. Very hard to hear. So you have to, every day of your lives, be ready to hear what whispers in your ear.

I'm not really interested in making money. That's always come as the result of success, but it's not been my goal, and I've had a tough time proving that to people.

The delicate balance of mentoring someone is not creating them in your own image, but giving them the opportunity to create themselves.

All of us every single year, we're a different person. I don't think we're the same person all our lives.

Whether in success or in failure, I'm proud of every single movie I've directed.

[50]

@TERRY CREWS

Actor and former professional football player

The reality is you get zero points for intentions.

You take action based on where you want to be, not based on where you are.

When you're coming up in the world, sometimes you've got to do things you don't enjoy.

I needed to be broken. Because the moment when you're broken is the moment when you can see what's really happening.

Every experience I have in my life begins in my head, and it's up to me to be positive, and learn, and grow, and make it all worthwhile.

Never let anyone define you. You are the only person who defines you. No one can speak for you. Only you speak for you. You are your only voice.

I decided everything was going to be a learning experience, and I was going to make good use of every single moment of every single day.

Once I began to have compassion for myself, and my family, and everyone I encounter, it changed everything.

If there was one thing I knew I wanted to do, it was grow, constantly, forever.

Dreams do come true. It takes a lot of work. But it can happen.

@TOM HARDY

Actor and producer

You mustn't be afraid to dream a little bigger, darling.

It doesn't matter who you are. What matters is your plan.

We are survivors. We control the fear. And without the fear, we are all as good as dead.

No matter how much you can prepare for it, there's nothing worse than the anticipation. It's always the killer of everything. The actuality of doing something is normally a lot easier than the waiting for it.

I'm not interested in walks in the parks. Anything difficult that people think I couldn't play, I'm straight at it. If they say "Tom, don't put your hand in the fire", you know I will be coming out of it casually an hour later with third-degree burns and bandages up to my arms.

We're all flawed human beings and we all have a cauldron of psychosis which we have to unravel as we grow older and find the way we fit in, to live our lives as best as possible.

Vanity is normal in performers. Does it bother other people? All the time. But nine times out of ten, that says more about them than you.

I have a very busy head. I have inside voices that I have learned to contain.

Spirituality seems to me to be for those who have been through hell.

There's always a certain pride in getting a job done properly.

@WILL SMITH

Grammy award winning actor

Life is lived on the edge.

The first step is you have to say that you can.

Money and success don't change people; they merely amplify what is already there.

Stop letting people who do so little for you control so much of your mind, feelings and emotions.

Too many people spend money they haven't earned, to buy things they don't want, to impress people they don't like.

Don't chase people. Be yourself, do your own thing and work hard. The right people — the ones who really belong in your life — will come to you. And stay.

Throughout life people will make you mad, disrespect you and treat you bad. Let God deal with the things they do, because hate in your heart will consume you too.

The separation of talent and skill is one of the greatest misunderstood concepts for people who are trying to excel, who have dreams, who want to do things. Talent you have naturally. Skill is only developed by hours and hours and hours of beating on your craft.

Fear is not real. The only place that fear can exist is in our thoughts of the future. It is a product of our imagination, causing us to fear things that do not at present and may not ever exist. Do not misunderstand me, danger is very real, but fear is a choice.

Life isn't how many breaths you take, but it's the moments that take your breath away.

I wake up every morning believing today is going to be better than yesterday.

Being realistic is the most commonly traveled road to mediocrity.

If you don't fight for what you want, don't cry for what you lost.

@WILLIAM SHAKESPEARE

Playwright, actor and poet

No legacy is so rich as honesty.

Love all, trust a few, do wrong to none.

Give every man thy ear, but few thy voice.

Have more than you show, speak less than you know.

If we are true to ourselves, we cannot be false to anyone.

A fool thinks himself to be wise, but a wise man knows himself to be a fool.

Like as the waves make towards the pebbled shore, so do our minutes hasten to their end.

Time is very slow for those who wait. Very fast for those who are scared. Very long for those who celebrate. But for those who love, time is eternal.

Love me or hate me, both are in my favor, if you love me, I'll always be in your heart, if you hate me, I'll always be in your mind.

There is nothing either good or bad but thinking makes it so.

Always the wrong person gives you the right lesson in life.

Don't waste your love on somebody, who doesn't value it.

We know what we are, but know not what we may be.

Expectation is the root of all heartache.

Make not your thoughts your prisons.

@YODA

Legendary character in Star Wars

We must wake.

You will find only what you bring in.

Control, control, you must learn control!

Difficult to see. Always in motion is the future.

In a dark place we find ourselves, and a little more knowledge lights our way.

If no mistake have you made, yet losing you are, a different game you should play.

Once you start down the dark path, forever will it dominate your destiny, consume you it will.

Attachment leads to jealousy. The shadow of greed, that is. Train yourself to let go of everything you fear to lose.

Fear is the path to the dark side. Fear leads to anger. Anger leads to hate. Hate leads to suffering.

In the end, cowards are those who follow the dark side.

No! Try not. Do, or do not. There is no try.

Always pass on what you have learned.

PART III

MUSIC

@ARETHA FRANKLIN

Singer, songwriter and civil rights activist

Every birthday is a gift. Every day is a gift.

Sometimes, what you're looking for is already there.

People really don't have to give you anything, so appreciate what people give you.

Trying to grow up is hurting. You make mistakes. You try to learn from them, and when you don't, it hurts even more.

Everybody wants respect. In their own way even three-year-olds would like respect, and acknowledgment, in their terms.

You cannot define a person on just one thing. You can't just forget all these wonderful and good things that a person has done because one thing didn't come off the way you thought it should come off.

Music does a lot of things for a lot of people. It's transporting, for sure. It can take you right back, it's uplifting, it's encouraging, it's strengthening.

Being a singer is a natural gift. It means I'm using to the highest degree possible the gift that God gave me to use. I'm happy with that.

It really is an honor if I can be inspirational to a younger singer or person. It means I've done my job.

Falling out of love is like losing weight. It's a lot easier putting it on than taking it off.

Who hasn't had a weight issue? If not the body, certainly the big head!

@BEYONCÉ KNOWLES-CARTER

Singer, songwriter, record producer, dancer and actress

Do what you were born to do. You have to trust yourself.

You can't appreciate the good times without the bad ones.

If everything was perfect, you would never learn and you would never grow.

The reality is: sometimes you lose. And you're never too good to lose. You're never too big to lose. You're never too smart to lose. It happens.

When you love and accept yourself, when you know who really cares about you, and when you learn from your mistakes, then you stop caring about what people who don't know you think.

I wanted to sell a million records, and I sold a million records. I wanted to go platinum; and I went platinum. I've been working nonstop since I was 15. I don't even know how to chill out.

I can never be safe; I always try and go against the grain. As soon as I accomplish one thing, I just set a higher goal. That's how I've gotten to where I am.

When I'm not feeling my best I ask myself, 'What are you gonna do about it?' I use the negativity to fuel the transformation into a better me.

Your self-worth is determined by you. You don't have to depend on someone telling you who you are.

I don't like to gamble, but if there's one thing I'm willing to bet on, it's myself.

With a lot of success comes a lot of negativity.

Power is not given to you. You have to take it.

@CAMERON 'WIZ KHALIFA' THOMAZ

Rapper, singer, songwriter and actor

Great minds think alone.

There are consequences to every decision.

Anything you want, you can get, you gotta build it though.

Everyone is born beautiful, some people just let the world turn them into something ugly.

Don't let the sadness from the past and the fear of the future, ruin the happiness of the present.

The most daring thing is to be yourself and to do exactly what you want to do at that point in time and not to be worried with what other people are doing or what's popular.

Girls fall in love with what they hear. Boys fall in love with what they see. That's why girls wear make-up and boys lie.

Be careful what you say to someone today. Because tomorrow they might not be here, and you can't take it back.

You don't need too many people to be happy. Just a few real ones who appreciate you for who you are.

Sometimes the best way to get someone's attention is to stop giving them yours.

Don't worry about someone who doesn't worry about you.

A day without a smile is a day wasted.

Good things come in good time.

@FRANK SINATRA

Singer, actor and producer

I'm gonna live till I die.

The best revenge is massive success.

Don't hide your scars. They make you who you are.

The big lesson in life, baby, is never be scared of anyone or anything.

If you possess something but you can't give it away, then you don't possess it, it possesses you.

I'm not one of those complicated, mixed-up cats. I'm not looking for the secret to life. I just go on from day to day, taking what comes.

I would like to be remembered as a man who had a wonderful time living life, a man who had good friends, fine family — and I don't think I could ask for anything more than that, actually.

I'm like Albert Schweitzer and Bertrand Russell and Albert Einstein in that I have a respect for life — in any form. I believe in nature, in the birds, the sea, the sky, in everything I can see or that there is real evidence for. If these things are what you mean by God, then I believe in God.

What I do with my life is of my own doing. I live it the best way I can. I've been criticized on many, many occasions, because of — acquaintances, and what have you.

You only go around once, but if you play your cards right, once is enough.

Alcohol may be man's worst enemy, but the bible says love your enemy.

Regrets, I've had a few; But then again, too few to mention.

I'm for whatever gets you through the night.

@JENNIFER LOPEZ

Singer, dancer, fashion designer and businesswoman

You mirror what the world mirrors to you.

Don't push your weaknesses, play with your strengths.

What you need to know is, nobody can save you or heal you. Only you can do that for you.

Sometimes you have to explore the darkness to get to the light and get back to who you are.

You've got to love yourself first. You've got to be okay on your own before you can be okay with somebody else.

Things don't always turn out exactly the way you want them to be and you feel disappointed. You are not always going to be the winner. That's when you have to stop and figure out why things happened the way they did and what you can do to change them.

Because the truth is, nobody knows what's best for you better than you do. You have to really sit still and ask yourself: What do I want? Does this feel right? What should I do? I realized I had to go back and do what I had always done. Listening to my gut was just as important as listening to the advice of others, and only I knew what was best for me.

There is a force in the world and an energy that you can put out, and when you put out love it comes back to you. I think that's my basic philosophy.

Beauty is only skin deep. I think what's really important is finding a balance of mind, body and spirit.

Ultimately, we can never change someone else's behavior—we can only change our own.

You get what you give. What you put into things is what you get out of them.

@JOHN LENNON

Singer, songwriter, peace activist and founder of The Beatles

Count your age by friends, not years. Count your life by smiles, not tears.

Being honest may not get you a lot of friends but it'll always get you the right ones.

If everyone demanded peace instead of another television set, then there'd be peace.

When you do something beautiful and nobody notices, do not be sad. For the sun, every morning is a beautiful spectacle and yet most of the audience still sleeps.

I believe that what people call God is something in all of us. I believe that what Jesus and Muhammad and Buddha and all the rest said was right. It's just that the translations have gone wrong.

There are two basic motivating forces: fear and love. When we are afraid, we pull back from life. When we are in love, we open to all that life has to offer with passion, excitement, and acceptance.

When I was 5 years old, my mother always told me that happiness was the key to life. When I went to school, they asked me what I wanted to be when I grew up. I wrote down 'happy'. They told me I didn't understand the assignment, and I told them they didn't understand life.

I believe in everything until it's disproved. So I believe in fairies, the myths, dragons. It all exists, even if it's in your mind. Who's to say that dreams and nightmares aren't as real as the here and now?

A dream you dream alone is only a dream. A dream you dream together is reality.

The more I see the less I know for sure.

Reality leaves a lot to the imagination.

@MADONNA LOUISE CICCONE

Singer, songwriter and actress

Express yourself, don't repress yourself.

I am my own experiment. I am my own work of art.

In the blink of an eye everything can change! Why waste time?

A lot of people are afraid to say what they want. That's why they don't get what they want.

No matter who you are, no matter what you did, no matter where you've come from, you can always change and become a better version of yourself.

I believe that we are at a very low level of consciousness, and we do not know how to treat each other as human beings. We are caught up in our own lives, our own needs, our own ego gratification. I feel a strong sense of responsibility in delivering that message.

With all the chaos, pain and suffering in the world, the fact that my adoption of a child who was living in an orphanage, you know, was the number one story for a week in the world. To me, that says more about our inability to focus on the real problems.

If you have children, you know you're responsible for somebody. You realize you are being imitated; your belief systems and priorities have a direct influence on these children, who are like flowers in a garden.

We learn our lessons; we get hurt; we want revenge. Then we realize that actually, happiness and forgiving people is the best revenge.

Poor is the man whose pleasures depend on the permission of another.

Better to live one year as a tiger, than a hundred as sheep.

If it's bitter at the start, then it's sweeter in the end.

@MARSHALL 'EMINEM' MATHERS

Rapper, songwriter and record producer

A normal life is boring.

You can make something of your life. It just depends on your drive.

I was poor white trash, no glitter, no glamour, but I'm not ashamed of anything.

Everybody has goals, aspirations or whatever, and everybody has been at a point in their life where nobody believed in them.

I didn't have nothin' going for me... school, home... until I found something I loved, which was music, and that changed everything.

When you're a little kid, you don't see color, and the fact that my friends were black never crossed my mind. It never became an issue until I was a teenager and started trying to rap.

I say what I want to say and do what I want to do. There's no in between. People will either love you for it or hate you for it.

The truth is you don't know what is going to happen tomorrow. Life is a crazy ride, and nothing is guaranteed.

I try to treat all the money I'm making like it's the last time I'm going to make it.

If you have enemies, good that means you stood up for something.

Behind every successful person lies a pack of haters.

Be proud of who you are.

@RAKIM 'A$AP ROCKY' MAYERS

Rapper, record producer, model and music video director

God is letting me shine, because I've got a good heart.

I'm a people's person, believe it or not. I just have a dark side to me, which we all do.

I want to inspire people to really open up their minds and not be one-sided or biased or hypocritical.

I don't care what straight people do, I don't care what gay people do. I don't care what nobody do. That's they business. I just care about what I do. You know what I'm saying?

I want to be the first guy to help people accept everybody for who they are. I'm talking about colors, religions, sex, everybody. My music is for everybody, it's not just for one kind of group.

I strive for perfection, but I'm not perfect. But what I can say is my morals are totally different than any other 24-year-old rapper my age now. I look at life totally different. A whole other aspect. I have different views and morals on life in general. And opinions.

I want to make my own path and leave behind a good legacy for myself and honestly, I just want to be innovative and always down for other people. That's what I want to be remembered by. I want to inspire.

I didn't want to be a loser, but I didn't want to fit in at the same time because I don't like just being ordinary. So it's one of those situations where I always kept my head up.

I thought highly of myself growing up. I still do. There's not really much somebody can say to me to bring down my confidence or anything.

@ROBYN RIHANNA FENTY

Singer, songwriter, actress and businesswoman

Don't hide from who you are.

Settling is the worst feeling in the world.

People gonna talk whether you doing good or bad.

Let go of the things that make you feel dead! Life is worth living!

The minute you learn to love yourself you won't want to be anyone else.

I think a lot of people are afraid of being happy because of what others might think.

You may never be good enough for everybody, but you will always be the best for somebody.

Sure, you wish you did some things differently. But there is no sense in becoming burdened with regret over things you have no power to change.

People think, because we're young, we aren't complex, but that's not true. We deal with life and love and broken hearts in the same way a woman a few years older might.

Nobody can understand what you're feeling unless they burn the way you burned.

It's nice to look back on your life and see things as lessons, and not regrets.

Keep your eyes on the finish line and not on the turmoil around you.

It's tougher to be vulnerable than to actually be tough.

Hurt me with the truth. Don't comfort me with a lie.

@SEAN 'DIDDY' COMBS

Rapper, record producer and entrepreneur

It's okay to be crazy, but don't be insane.

You have to be somewhat crazy if you want to be successful.

If you want to fly, you have to give up the things that weigh you down.

Set some goals. Stay quiet about them. Smash the hell out of them. Clap for your damn self.

I think that you have to believe. That's one of my biggest mantras, is believe. I wouldn't be here if I didn't believe in myself.

I want to convey how beautiful it is to close your eyes and dream. And then to open them and make that dream a reality.

People from all walks of life and all over the world look at me and know my humble beginnings and know that everything I've done has been through hard work. People respect me as a marketer and brand builder.

I have learned to enjoy the ups for what they are because those are the moments that feel like they go by the quickest.

Success doesn't just land on your lap, you have to work, work, work, work and work some more.

Everyone has challenges and lessons to learn — we wouldn't be who we are without them.

You cannot achieve success without failure.

It always seems impossible until it's done.

@SHAWN 'JAY Z' CARTER

Rapper, record producer and entrepreneur

I believe you can speak things into existence.

My first album didn't come out until I was 26.

The genius thing we did was, we didn't give up.

I love what I do, and when you love what you do, you want to be the best at it.

Belief in oneself and knowing who you are, I mean, that's the foundation for everything great.

Life is all there is. And if that's true, then we have to really live it — we have to take it for everything it is and 'die enormous' instead of 'living dormant.'

Excellence is being able to perform at a high level over and over again. You can hit a half-court shot once. That's just the luck of the draw. If you consistently do it, that's excellence.

I'm a mirror. If you're cool with me, I'm cool with you, and the exchange starts. What you see is what you reflect. If you don't like what you see, then you've done something. If I'm standoffish, that's because you are.

Identity is a prison you can never escape, but the way to redeem your past is not to run from it, but to try to understand it, and use it as a foundation to grow.

A wise man told me don't argue with fools. Cause people from a distance can't tell who is who.

Money and power don't change you, they just further expose your true self.

A man who doesn't take care of his family, can't be rich.

If you can't buy it twice you can't afford it.

@TUPAC '2PAC' SHAKUR

Regarded as one of the most influential rappers of all time

People die but legends live forever.

Life is a wheel of fortune and it's my turn to spin it.

I would rather be stricken blind, than to live without expression of mind.

Everytime I speak, I want the truth to come out. Everytime I speak I want a shiver.

Pay no mind to those who talk behind your back, it simply means that you are two steps ahead.

You gotta make a change. You see the old way wasn't working so it's on us, to do what we gotta do to survive.

I'm not saying I'm gonna change the world, but I guarantee that I will create a spark in the brain that will change the world.

Death is not the greatest loss in life. The greatest loss is what dies inside while still alive. Never surrender.

All I'm trying to do is survive and make good out of the dirty, nasty, unbelievable lifestyle that they gave me.

I mean why have 52 rooms and you know there's somebody with no room? It just don't make sense to me.

Everybody's at war with different things. I'm at war with my own heart sometimes.

During your life, never stop dreaming. No one can take away your dreams.

Just cause you live in the ghetto doesn't mean you can't grow.

PART IV
BUSINESS

@ALEXANDER GRAHAM BELL

Engineer, scientist and inventor of the first telephone

Before anything else, preparation is the key to success.

You cannot force ideas. Successful ideas are the result of slow growth.

Concentrate all your thoughts upon the work at hand. The sun's rays do not burn until brought to focus.

The day will come when the man at the telephone will be able to see the distant person to whom he is speaking to.

Leave the beaten track behind occasionally and dive into the woods. Every time you do you will be certain to find something you have never seen before.

Great discoveries and improvements invariably involve the cooperation of many minds. I may be given credit for having blazed the trail, but when I look at the subsequent developments I feel the credit is due to others rather than to myself.

What this power is I cannot say; all I know is that it exists and it becomes available only when a man is in that state of mind in which he knows exactly what he wants and is fully determined not to quit until he finds it.

I would impress upon your minds the fact that if you want to do a man justice, you should believe what a man says himself rather than what people say he says.

Educate the masses, elevate their standard of intelligence, and you will certainly have a successful nation.

A man, as a general rule, owes very little to what he is born with — a man is what he makes of himself.

The achievement of one goal should be the starting point of another.

@ALFRED NOBEL

Businessman, chemist and inventor famous for holding the patent for dynamite

Contentment is the only real wealth.

If I have a thousand ideas and only one turns out to be good, I am satisfied.

I would not leave anything to a man of action as he would be tempted to give up work; on the other hand, I would like to help dreamers as they find it difficult to get on in life.

I regard large inherited wealth as a misfortune, which merely serves to dull men's faculties. A man who possesses great wealth should, therefore, allow only a small portion to descend to his relatives. Even if he has children, I consider it a mistake to hand over to them considerable sums of money beyond what is necessary for their education. To do so merely encourages laziness and impedes the healthy development of the individual's capacity to make an independent position for himself.

Nature is man's teacher. She unfolds her treasures to his search, unseals his eye, illumes his mind, and purifies his heart; an influence breathes from all the sights and sounds of her existence.

One can state, without exaggeration, that the observation of and the search for similarities and differences are the basis of all human knowledge.

Lawyers have to make a living, and can only do so by inducing people to believe that a straight line is crooked.

A heart can no more be forced to love than a stomach can be forced to digest food by persuasion.

Worry is the stomach's worst poison.

@ANDREW CARNEGIE

Industrialist and philanthropist

Anything worth having is worth working for.

Do your duty and a little more and the future will take care of itself.

As I grow older, I pay less attention to what men say. I just watch what they do.

Wealth is not to feed the egos but to feed the hungry and to help people help themselves.

If you want to be happy, set a goal that commands your thoughts, liberates your energy, and inspires your hopes.

Every act you have ever performed since the day you were born was performed because you wanted something.

People who are unable to motivate themselves must be content with mediocrity, no matter how impressive their other talents.

The average person puts only 25% of his energy and ability into his work. The world takes off its hat to those who put in more than 50% of their capacity, and stands on its head for those few and far between souls who devote 100%.

Immense power is acquired by assuring yourself in your secret reveries that you were born to control affairs.

You cannot push anyone up a ladder unless he is willing to climb a little himself.

All human beings can alter their lives by altering their attitudes.

No man can become rich without himself enriching others.

There is little success where there is little laughter.

It is the mind that makes the body rich.

@ARIANNA HUFFINGTON

Entrepreneur, author and co-founder of The Huffington Post

Life is a dance between making it happen and letting it happen.

You have to do what you dream of doing even while you're afraid.

We have if we're lucky about 30,000 days to play the game of life. How we play it will be determined by what we value.

Fearlessness is like a muscle. I know from my own life that the more I exercise it the more natural it becomes to not let my fears run me.

The quest for knowledge is pursued at higher speeds with smarter tools today, but wisdom is found no more readily than it was three thousand years ago in the court of King Solomon.

Success is commonly defined as money and power, but increasingly that's not enough. It's almost like a two-legged stool where you fall over if that's all you measure your life by.

To live the lives we truly want and deserve, and not just the lives we settle for, we need a third measure of success that goes beyond money and power, and consists of four pillars: well-being, wisdom, wonder, and giving.

We think mistakenly, that success is the result of the amount of the time we put in at work, instead of the quality of the time we put in.

We need to accept that we won't always make the right decisions sometimes and that we'll screw up royally sometimes.

Failure is not the opposite of success; it's part of success.

@AUBREY MARCUS

Entrepreneur, founder of ONNIT and author of Own The Day, Own Your Life

To wait for the external world to change before you alleviate your stress is a fool's errand.

See your future. I want you to imagine yourself a year from now. You know that in a year you are going to be different, whether you do nothing or something. And the choices you make between now and then will determine that difference.

As humans we desire to apply our force—our work—to the maximum effect possible. Our mission is what we want that force to accomplish. While the meaning of life might be complicated, your mission in life should not be complicated. What are you, in this lifetime, on this planet, in this body, here to do? What do you want more than anything else?

Time is the wrong metric to use when we evaluate work. Because it's not just about how much time you work, it's about how effectively you use that time.

To live one day well is the same as to live ten thousand days well. To master twenty-four hours is to master your life.

Small things, when compounded over time, tend to have big consequences.

You are not rewarded for the comfortable choice.

It's not where you begin, it's where you end.

@BILL GATES

Business magnate, software developer, philanthropist and co-founder of Microsoft

Your most unhappy customers are your greatest source of learning.

We all need people who will give us feedback. That's how we improve.

The Internet is becoming the town square for the global village of tomorrow.

Success is a lousy teacher. It seduces smart people into thinking they can't lose.

It's fine to celebrate success but it is more important to heed the lessons of failure.

Don't compare yourself with anyone in this world — if you do so, you are insulting yourself.

I choose a lazy person to do a hard job. Because a lazy person will find an easy way to do it.

I really had a lot of dreams when I was a kid, and I think a great deal of that grew out of the fact that I had a chance to read a lot.

The belief that the world is getting worse, that we can't solve extreme poverty and disease, isn't just mistaken. It is harmful.

I believe that if you show people the problems and you show them the solutions they will be moved to act.

As we look ahead into the next century, leaders will be those who empower others.

The general idea of the rich helping the poor, I think, is important.

We have got to put a lot of money into changing behavior.

Treatment without prevention is simply unsustainable.

@BOB PROCTOR

Entrepreneur, motivational speaker and author of Born Rich

Change is inevitable but personal growth is a choice.

Stay in charge of you, don't let the outside world control you.

The only competition you will ever face is with your own ignorance.

Thoughts become things. If you see it in your mind, you will hold it in your hand.

Faith and fear both demand you believe in something you cannot see. You choose.

You don't decide what your purpose in life is, you discover it. Your purpose is your reason for living.

Set a goal to achieve something that is so big, so exhilarating that it excites you and scares you at the same time.

No amount of reading or memorizing will make you successful in life. It is the understanding and application of wise thought that counts.

Gratitude is an attitude that hooks us up to our source of supply. And the more grateful you are, the closer you become to your maker, to the architect of the universe, to the spiritual core of your being. It's a phenomenal lesson.

See yourself living in abundance and you will attract it. It always works, it works every time with every person.

The Subconscious mind can not tell the difference between what's real and what's imagined.

What do you want? Sit down and write it out on a piece of paper. Write it in the present tense.

It doesn't matter where you are, you are nowhere compared to where you can go.

The only limits in our life are those we impose on ourselves.

Be like a postage stamp. Stick to it until you get there.

@CARLOS SLIM HELU

Business magnate, investor and philanthropist

The biggest things in life are not materials.

All times are good times for those who know how to work and have the tools to do so.

Live the present intensely and fully, do not let the past be a burden, and let the future be an incentive. Each person forges his or her own destiny.

Do not allow negative feelings and emotions to control your mind. Emotional harm does not come from others; it is conceived and developed within ourselves.

The truth is, you leave this world with nothing. What you are is a temporary administrator, and you must administer well the wealth in your care, and generate more. The surplus can be used to do many things for people.

With a good perspective of history we can have a better understanding of the past and present, and thus a clear vision of the future.

It's important to give a better country to your children, but it is more important to give better children to your country.

When we face our problems, they disappear. So learn from failure and let success be the silent incentive.

Mistakes are normal and human. Make them small, accept them, correct them, and forget them.

Firm and patient optimism always yields its rewards.

@CHARLIE MUNGER

Investor, philanthropist and vice chairman of Berkshire Hathaway

Those who keep learning, will keep rising in life.

Spend each day trying to be a little wiser than you were when you woke up.

The best thing a human being can do is to help another human being know more.

Assume life will be really tough, and then ask if you can handle it. If the answer is yes, you've won.

In my whole life, I have known no wise people (over a broad subject matter area) who didn't read all the time — none, zero.

I've got some advice for the young: If you've got anything you really want to do, don't wait until you're 93.

If you're unhappy with what you've had over the last 50 years, you have an unfortunate misappraisal of life. It's as good as it gets, and it's very likely to get worse.

To get what you want, you have to deserve what you want. The world is not yet a crazy enough place to reward a whole bunch of undeserving people.

Do the best you can do. Never tell a lie. If you say you're going to do it, get it done. Nobody cares about an excuse.

You must force yourself to consider opposing arguments. Especially when they challenge your best loved ideas.

If you can get really good at destroying your own wrong ideas, that is a great gift.

I would argue that passion is more important than brain power.

There's only one way to the top: hard work.

@DAN PEÑA

Entrepreneur and business coach

Don't waste time on things you can't change.

We all have baggage from our upbringing! That's life!

Life without dreams is like a bird with a broken wing — it can't fly.

Entrepreneurship is enduring pain for a long time without relinquishing.

Wishing, hoping, and dreaming without an action plan — is nothing more than a pipe dream.

There's no seminar in the world that will give you multi million-dollar advice on building a business from scratch.

If you want to make more money, you'll have to do things differently. You will have to do things you never even thought of doing in the past. You will have to do things out of your comfort zone.

Remarkably successful people habitually do what other people won't do. They go where others won't go because there's a lot less competition and a much greater chance for success.

Your most valuable natural asset is your own gut instinct. Don't be afraid of it, your instinct has more power than all of the conventional wisdom in the world.

If you don't embrace a workload others would consider crazy, then your goal doesn't mean that much to you.

High performance people take action quickly and change their mind slowly.

The more you investigate, the less you have to invest.

Tough times don't last — tough people do!

@DANA WHITE

Businessman and president of the UFC

I love doing things that people say can't be done.

I'm a guy who did exactly what he wanted to do. When you do that, the money follows.

It was never about the money for me, it was about doing something that I loved, it was more about passion.

The amount of negativity I hear on a daily basis is unbelievable. But that's the kind of stuff you have to tune out, focus, stick with your vision and keep plugging every day.

Anything can be changed. Anything can be fixed. Things that are broken can be fixed. And you don't have to be some billionaire or millionaire to do it. You just have to be a person with a vision and the passion to do it, and be willing to fight for it every day.

Whatever it is that you're passionate about, whatever it is that you absolutely love, and whatever it is that you would get up out of bed every day and do for free, you should try to figure out a way to make money at it and give it a shot.

Don't be that guy that's laying in that hospital bed going, 'I wonder what would have happened if I tried it?' The worst thing that could happen is that it doesn't work.

My legacy to me is when I drop dead and they're at my funeral — I want my three kids to get up and say, 'He's an awesome dad'.

@DAVID GOGGINS

Retired Navy SEAL, ultramarathon runner and author of Can't Hurt Me

To grow in life, be willing to suffer.

You have to be willing to go to war with yourself and create a whole new identity.

When you're in hell, you forget how great you really are because you're suffering and you forget the great things you've done.

The mind is the most powerful thing in the world. The mind has capabilities that are so unknown, and being able to tap into that is on the other side of suffering.

Our whole life is set up in the path of least resistance. We don't want to suffer. We don't want to feel discomfort. So the whole time, we're living our lives in a very comfortable area. There's no growth in that.

A lot of us have a dialogue that is crap. It's a crappy dialogue. We live in a world right now that is very external. Everything is very on the surface. Superficial. Everything. And what we're telling ourselves is what we see on TV.

The things that we decide to run from are the truth. When you make excuses, you're running from the truth.

You gotta start your journey. It may suck, but eventually you will come out the other side on top.

Life is one big tug of war between mediocrity and trying to find your best self.

Self-talk and visualization are the keys to fighting negativity.

Don't live in an external world, go inside yourself.

Admit your weaknesses.

@DAYMOND JOHN

Businessman, investor, founder and CEO of FUBU

The easiest thing to sell is the truth.

If you really want something, stop chasing it.

Don't focus on you, focus on what you can give others.

If people haven't laughed at your dreams, then you aren't dreaming big enough, just keep pushing forward.

Don't wait for the 'perfect time', you will wait forever. Always take advantage of the time that you're given.

Everyone has an idea, but it's taking those first steps toward turning that idea into a reality that is always the toughest.

If you don't educate yourself, you'll never get out of the starting block because you'll spend all your money making foolish decisions.

Learn as many mistakes and what not to do while your business or product is small. Don't be in such a hurry to grow your brand. Make sure that you and the market can sustain any bumps that may occur down the road.

Five days a week, I read my goals before I go to sleep and when I wake up. There are 10 goals around health, family, and business with expiration dates, and I update them every six months.

I believe the last thing I read at night will likely manifest when I'm sleeping. You become what you think about the most.

Success is waking up every day and doing what you want to do.

Mentors by far, are the most important aspects of businesses.

As an entrepreneur, you never stop learning.

I've failed way more than I've succeeded.

@ELON MUSK

Entrepreneur, investor and founder of PayPal and SpaceX

Life is too short for long-term grudges.

I think it matters whether someone has a good heart.

The first step is to establish that something is possible then probability will occur.

When something is important enough, you do it even if the odds are not in your favor.

I think we have a duty to maintain the light of consciousness to make sure it continues Into the future.

People should pursue what they're passionate about. That will make them happier than pretty much anything else.

I think that's the single best piece of advice: constantly think about how you could be doing things better and questioning yourself.

When Henry Ford made cheap, reliable cars people said, 'Nah, what's wrong with a horse?' That was a huge bet he made, and it worked.

If you get up in the morning and think the future is going to be better, it's a bright day. Otherwise, it's not.

I take the position that I'm always to some degree wrong, and the aspiration is to be less wrong.

Some people don't like change, but you need to embrace change if the alternative is disaster.

Persistence is very important. You should not give up unless you are forced to give up.

You get paid in direct proportion to the difficulty of the problems you solve.

I think it is possible for ordinary people to choose to be extraordinary.

Patience is a virtue, and I'm learning patience. It's a tough lesson.

@GABRIELLE 'COCO' CHANEL

Entrepreneur, fashion designer and founder of Chanel

Simplicity is the keynote of all true elegance.

Elegance is when the inside is as beautiful as the outside.

The most courageous act is still to think for yourself. Aloud.

Don't spend time beating on a wall, hoping to transform it into a door.

Nature gives you the face you have at twenty; it is up to you to merit the face you have at fifty.

I am not young but I feel young. The day I feel old, I will go to bed and stay there. J'aime la vie! I feel that to live is a wonderful thing.

Fashion is not something that exists in dresses only. Fashion is in the sky, in the street, fashion has to do with ideas, the way we live, what is happening.

I invented my life by taking for granted that everything I did not like would have an opposite, which I would like.

Those who create are rare; those who cannot are numerous. Therefore, the latter are stronger.

How many cares one loses when one decides not to be something but to be someone.

Success is most often achieved by those who don't know that failure is inevitable.

In order to be irreplaceable one must always be different.

A girl should be two things: who and what she wants.

My life didn't please me, so I created my life.

@GARY VAYNERCHUCK

Entrepreneur, internet personality and author of Crushing It

Skills are cheap. Passion is priceless.

Without hustle, your talent will only get you so far.

When it comes down to it, nothing trumps execution.

Do the work. Everyone wants to be successful, but nobody wants to do the work.

Life shrinks and expands on the proportion of your willingness to take risks and try new things.

You are not patient enough. Your lack of patience is killing you and your need of things is killing you.

I hate how many people think "glass half-empty" when their glass is really four-fifths full. I'm grateful when I have one drop in the glass because I know exactly what to do with it.

People are chasing cash, not happiness. When you chase money, you're going to lose. You're just going to. Even if you get the money, you're not going to be happy.

The reason we love our parents is because they loved us first. Every single company should take this advice.

I put zero weight into anyone's opinion about me because I know exactly who I am.

Your legacy is being written by yourself. Make the right decisions.

Time — the one asset none of us are ever going to get more of.

We only get to play this game one time. We have one life.

Legacy is greater than currency.

@HENRY FORD

Industrialist, business magnate and founder of the Ford Motor Company

Quality means doing it right when no one is looking.

If you think you can do a thing or think you can't do a thing, you're right.

Thinking is the hardest work there is, which is probably the reason why so few engage in it.

Anyone who stops learning is old, whether at twenty or eighty. Anyone who keeps learning stays young. The greatest thing in life is to keep your mind young.

If there is any one secret of success, it lies in the ability to get the other person's point of view and see things from that person's angle as well as from your own.

Enthusiasm is the yeast that makes your hopes shine to the stars. Enthusiasm is the sparkle in your eyes, the swing in your gait. The grip of your hand, the irresistible surge of will and energy to execute your ideas.

If money is your hope for independence, you will never have it. The only real security that a man can have in this world is a reserve of knowledge, experience and ability.

One of the greatest discoveries a person makes, one of their great surprises, is to find they can do what they were afraid they couldn't do.

When everything seems to be going against you, remember that the airplane takes off against the wind, not with it.

It has been my observation that most people get ahead during the time that others waste.

Failure is simply the opportunity to begin again, this time more intelligently.

You can't build a reputation on what you are going to do.

Don't find fault, find a remedy; anybody can complain.

@HOWARD SCHULTZ

Former CEO of Starbucks and author of Onward

Whatever you do, don't play it safe.

Don't be threatened by people smarter than you.

You have to have 100% belief in your core reason for being.

In times of adversity and change, we really discover who we are and what we're made of.

I believe life is a series of near misses. A lot of what we ascribe to luck is not luck at all, it's seizing the day and accepting responsibility for your future. It's seeing what other people don't see and pursuing that vision.

You've got to be truthful. I don't think you should be vulnerable every day, but there are moments where you've got to share your soul and conscience with people and show them who you are, and not be afraid of it.

We have no patent on anything we do and anything we do can be copied by anyone else. But you can't copy the heart and soul and the conscience of the company.

In life, you can blame a lot of people and you can wallow in self-pity, or you can pick yourself up and say, listen, I have to be responsible for myself.

I feel so strongly that the reason I'm here is I dreamed big dreams. I dreamed the kind of dreams that other people said would not be possible.

In anything we do, any endeavour, it's not what you do; it's why you do it.

Success is empty if you arrive at the finish line alone.

@JACK DORSEY

Entrepreneur, computer programmer and co-founder of Twitter

Question every little thing.

Build what you want to see in this world.

Short term satisfaction will never lead to something timeless.

Make every detail perfect, and limit the number of details to perfect.

You can worry about the competition or you can focus on what's ahead of you and drive fast.

Everyone has an idea. But it's really about executing the idea and attracting other people to help you work on the idea.

The strongest thing you can cultivate as an entrepreneur is to not rely on luck but cultivating an ability to recognize fortunate situations when they are occurring.

I spend 90% of my time with people who don't report to me, which also allows for serendipity, since I'm walking around the office all the time. You don't have to schedule serendipity. It just happens.

The greatest lesson that I learned in all of this is that you have to start. Start now, start here, start small and keep it simple.

Great companies don't just have one founding moment. They have many founding moments.

Starting anything is a roller coaster with the highest highs and lowest lows.

Expect the unexpected. And whenever possible, be the unexpected.

Success is never accidental.

@JACK MA

Business magnate, investor, philanthropist and co-founder of Alibaba Group

Opportunities lie in the place where the complaints are.

You should learn from your competitor, but never copy. Copy and you die.

If there are nine rabbits on the ground, if you want to catch one, just focus on one.

Never give up. Today is hard, tomorrow will be worse, but the day after tomorrow will be sunshine.

It doesn't matter if I failed. At least I passed the concept on to others. Even if I don't succeed, someone will succeed.

Help young people. Help small guys. Because small guys will be big. Young people will have the seeds you bury in their minds, and when they grow up, they will change the world.

I think the younger generation is always better than the last generation. No matter if you like it or not. My father said, 'Jack, I'm so good, you'll never be' — but I'm better than him. My father is better than my grandfather. My children will be better than us.

Today making money is very simple. But making sustainable money while being responsible to society and improving the world is very difficult.

Once in your life, try something. Work hard at something. Try to change. Nothing bad can happen.

The world will not remember what you say, but it will not forget what you have done.

If you've never tried, how will you ever know if there's any chance?

@JEFF BEZOS

Entrepreneur, investor and founder of Amazon

What's dangerous is not to evolve.

If you want to be inventive, you have to be willing to fail.

The human brain is an incredible pattern-matching machine.

I knew that if I failed I wouldn't regret that, but I knew the one thing I might regret is not trying.

One of the huge mistakes people make is that they try to force an interest on themselves. You don't choose your passions. Your passions choose you.

If you're not stubborn, you'll give up on experiments too soon. And if you're not flexible, you'll pound your head against the wall and you won't see a different solution to a problem you're trying to solve.

When the world changes around you and when it changes against you, what used to be a tail wind is now a head wind, you have to lean into that and figure out what to do because complaining isn't a strategy.

If you decide that you're going to do only the things you know are going to work, you're going to leave a lot of opportunity on the table.

A brand for a company is like a reputation for a person. You earn a reputation by trying to do hard things well.

Your brand is what other people say about you when you're not in the room.

Patience, persistence, and obsessive attention to detail.

What we need to do is always look into the future.

Be stubborn on vision but flexible on details.

@JIM ROHN

Entrepreneur, author and motivational speaker

Either you run the day, or the day runs you.

Work harder on yourself than you do on your job.

Take care of your body. It's the only place you have to live.

Motivation is what gets you started. Habit is what keeps you going.

You have two choices: You can make a living, or you can design a life.

Don't let your learning lead to knowledge. Let your learning lead to action.

Success is nothing more than a few simple disciplines, practiced every day.

You cannot change your destination overnight, but you can change your direction overnight.

If you don't design your own life plan, chances are you'll fall into someone else's plan. And guess what they have planned for you? Not much.

Start reading, and especially read the kinds of books that will help you unleash your inner potential.

We must all suffer one of two things: the pain of discipline or the pain of regret and disappointment.

The major value in life is not what you get. The major value in life is what you become.

Formal education will make you a living; self-education will make you a fortune.

If you are not willing to risk the unusual, you will have to settle for the ordinary.

Giving is better than receiving because giving starts the receiving process.

Discipline is the bridge between goals and accomplishment.

Money is usually attracted, not pursued.

@JOCKO WILLINK

Retired Navy SEAL, podcaster and author of Extreme Ownership

Ego clouds and disrupts everything.

If you get your ego in your way, you will only look to other people and circumstances to blame.

We all have a tendency to avoid our weaknesses. When we do that, we never progress or get any better.

To implement real change, to drive people to accomplish something truly complex or difficult or dangerous — you can't make people do these things. You have to lead them.

One of the key qualities a leader must possess is the ability to detach from the chaos, mayhem, and emotions in a situation and make good, clear decisions based on what is actually happening.

We have food all around us all the time, and if we haven't eaten for three hours, we think we're starving. You're not starving — human beings can go for 30 days without food.

Freedom is what everyone wants — to be able to act and live with freedom. But the only way to get to a place of freedom is through discipline.

The test is not a complex one: when the alarm goes off, do you get up out of bed, or do you lie there in comfort and fall back to sleep?

If you allow the status quo to persist, you can't expect to improve performance, and you can't expect to win.

Jiu Jitsu is probably the number one activity that I could recommend to someone to improve their lives overall.

When things are going bad, there's going to be some good that's going to come from it.

Discipline equals freedom.

@JOHN PIERPONT MORGAN

Financier and banker

You can't unscramble eggs.

When a man abuses his power, he loses it.

You can't pick cherries with your back to the trees.

My first guess is sometimes right. My second never is.

When you expect things to happen — strangely enough — they do happen.

The first step towards getting somewhere is to decide that you are not going to stay where you are.

The key to living a moral life is this: Do nothing in private that you would be ashamed to discuss openly with your mother.

No problem can be solved until it is reduced to some simple form. The changing of a vague difficulty into a specific, concrete form is a very essential element in thinking.

The wise man bridges the gap by laying out the path by means of which he can get from where he is to where he wants to go.

Nothing so undermines your financial judgement as the sight of your neighbor getting rich.

A man always has two reasons for doing anything: a good reason and the real reason.

Go as far as you can see; when you get there, you'll be able to see farther.

If you have to ask how much it costs, you can't afford it.

Millionaires don't use astrology, billionaires do.

@KEVIN O'LEARY

Businessman, author and TV personality

Money equals freedom.

Nobody has a monopoly on good ideas.

I like to take risks. That's how I make money. But they are calculated risks.

What matters is that you achieve success and become free. Then you can do whatever you like.

I have had some great successes and great failures. I think every entrepreneur has. I try to learn from all of them.

There is a discipline required as an entrepreneur about working to optimize the business. There is no balance in life as an entrepreneur. You can't expect to work 9 to 5 that's never going to happen. You have to expect that it is going to consume your life for a period of time. That's the downside, but the upside is that you buy yourself freedom in perpetuity.

When you're 21 years old or 20 or 18 or 19 and you start putting aside 10% of what you make, you'll have over $1,000,000 by the time you're 65. If no one else is going to worry about your retirement, I want you to worry about it.

I'd rather invest in an entrepreneur who has failed before, than one who assumes success from day one.

If you can't even acknowledge your failures, how can you cut the rope and move on?

We need physical exercise to prepare our brain for long periods of concentration.

@KEVIN SYSTROM

Entrepreneur, computer programmer and co-founder of Instagram

The world runs on luck.

Great products sell themselves.

Focusing on one thing and doing it really, really well can get you very far.

People always told me photos have been done. My feeling was, these people are wrong.

I promise you, a lot of it is luck. But you make your own luck by working really hard and trying lots and lots of things.

Everyone gets lucky for some amount in their life. And the question is, are you alert enough to know you're being lucky or you're becoming lucky?

If you've got an idea, start today. There's no better time than now to get going. That doesn't mean quit your job and jump into your idea 100% from day one, but there's always small progress that can be made to start the movement.

I'm always in awe of people who are artists in their fields — people who understand that simply by taking ideas and translating them into reality, they've created value in the world.

I don't think you should ever start a business and move in a direction where you can't see it becoming a business.

There's real beauty in pushing yourself to expose the real you in more ways.

You need to fail in order to find the right solution.

The best feature is less features.

@LARRY PAGE

Entrepreneur, computer scientist and co-founder of Google

Always deliver more than expected.

My goal is for Google to lead, not follow.

Always work hard on something uncomfortably exciting.

If you're not doing some things that are crazy, then you're doing the wrong things.

Anything you can imagine probably is doable, you just have to imagine it and work on it.

Optimism is important. You have to be a little silly about the goals you are going to set. You should try to do things that most people would not do.

For a lot of companies, it's useful for them to feel like they have an obvious competitor and to rally around that. I personally believe it's better to shoot higher. You don't want to be looking at your competitors. You want to be looking at what's possible and how to make the world better.

Lots of companies don't succeed over time. What do they fundamentally do wrong? They usually miss the future.

If we were motivated by money, we would have sold the company a long time ago and ended up on a beach.

The only way you are going to have success is to have lots of failures first.

It's very hard to fail completely if you aim high enough.

You never lose a dream, it just incubates as a hobby.

Have a healthy disregard for the impossible.

@MARISSA MAYER

Entrepreneur, investor and former CEO of Yahoo

You have to ruthlessly prioritize.

If you're the smartest person in the room, you're in the wrong room.

Do something you're not ready to do. In the worst case, you'll learn your limitations.

If you push through that feeling of being scared, that feeling of taking risk, really amazing things can happen.

Vince Lombardi says, you know, "In my life, there are three things: God, family and the Green Bay Packers, in that order. For me, it's God, family and Yahoo, in that order.

I always did something I was a little not ready to do. I think that's how you grow. When there's that moment of 'Wow, I'm not really sure I can do this,' and you push through those moments, that's when you have a breakthrough.

New beginnings — professional, personal, or come what may — are always uncomfortable, but being open to them is the only way to grow. In the end, we are all capable of so much more than we think.

I think it's very comforting for people to put me in a box. 'Oh, she's a fluffy girlie girl who likes clothes and cupcakes. Oh, but wait, she is spending her weekends doing hardware electronics.'

If you can find something that you're really passionate about, whether you're a man or a woman comes a lot less into play. Passion is a gender-neutralizing force.

Geeks are people who love something so much that all the details matter.

@MARK ZUCKERBERG

Entrepreneur, philanthropist and co-founder of Facebook

It takes courage to choose hope over fear.

Some people dream of success, while others wake up and work hard at it.

It is important for young entrepreneurs to be adequately self-aware to know what they do not know.

Books allow you to fully explore a topic and immerse yourself in a deeper way than most media today.

People can be really smart or have skills that are directly applicable, but if they don't really believe in it, then they are not going to really work hard.

The question I ask myself like almost every day is, 'Am I doing the most important thing I could be doing?' Unless I feel like I'm working on the most important problem that I can help with, then I'm not going to feel good about how I'm spending my time.

If you just work on stuff that you like and you're passionate about, you don't have to have a master plan with how things will play out.

My goal was never to just create a company. It was to build something that actually makes a really big change in the world.

By giving people the power to share, we're making the world more transparent.

People don't care about what you say, they care about what you build.

Instead of building walls, we can help build bridges.

@NAVAL RAVIKANT

Entrepreneur, investor and co-founder of AngelList

Earn with your mind, not your time.

You're never going to get rich renting out your time.

If you see a get rich quick scheme, that's someone else trying to get rich off of you.

This is such a short and precious life that it's really important that you don't spend it being unhappy.

A fit body, a calm mind, a house full of love. These things cannot be bought — they must be earned.

All the benefits in life come from compound interest — money, relationships, habits — anything of importance.

Knowledge is a skyscraper. You can take a shortcut with a fragile foundation of memorization, or build slowly upon a steel frame of understanding.

Doctors won't make you healthy. Nutritionists won't make you slim. Teachers won't make you smart. Gurus won't make you calm. Mentors won't make you rich. Trainers won't make you fit. Ultimately, you have to take responsibility. Save yourself.

Social media has degenerated into a deafening cacophony of groups signaling and repeating their shared myths.

The first rule of handling conflict is don't hang around people who are constantly engaging in conflict.

You have to surrender, at least a little bit, to be the best version of yourself possible.

Watch every thought. Always ask, why am I having this thought?

If you don't love yourself who will?

@NIKOLA TESLA

Inventor, mechanical and electrical engineer

We are all one.

It's not the love you make. It's the love you give.

Anti-social behaviour is a trait of intelligence in a world full of conformists.

If you want to find the secrets of the universe, think in terms of energy, frequency, and vibration.

We crave for new sensations but soon become indifferent to them. The wonders of yesterday are today common occurrences.

The spread of civilisation may be likened to a fire; first, a feeble spark, next a flickering flame, then a mighty blaze, ever increasing in speed and power.

My brain is only a receiver, in the Universe, there is a core from which we obtain knowledge, strength and inspiration. I have not penetrated into the secrets of this core, but I know that it exists.

The scientists of today think deeply instead of clearly. One must be sane to think clearly, but one can think deeply and be quite insane.

Misunderstandings are always caused by the inability of appreciating one another's point of view.

I do not think you can name many great inventions that have been made by married men.

Be alone, that is the secret of invention; be alone, that is when ideas are born.

Peace can only come as a natural consequence of universal enlightenment.

@PHIL KNIGHT

Business magnate, philanthropist and co-founder of Nike

Make history or be a part of it.

It's alright to be Goliath but always act like David.

Dare to take chances, lest you leave your talent buried in the ground.

When you really understand who you are, it enables you to fight and believe.

Any entrepreneur has to prepare for a lot of dark days, and they've got to really like what they are doing, and they have to have a reason for it to succeed.

There is an immutable conflict at work in life and in business, a constant battle between peace and chaos. Neither can be mastered, but both can be influenced. How you go about that is the key to success.

We wanted Nike to be the world's best sports and fitness company. Once you say that, you have a focus. You don't end up making wing tips or sponsoring the next Rolling Stones world tour.

Dream audaciously. Have the courage to fail forward. Act with urgency.

The cowards never started and the weak died along the way.

We knew we could fail; we just didn't think we would.

You only have to succeed the last time.

@RAY DALIO

Hedge fund manager, philanthropist and author of Principles

Treat your life like a game.

Listening to uninformed people is worse than having no answers at all.

If your objective is to be as good, as you can be, then you're going to want criticism.

You must not let your need to be right be more important than your need to find out what's true.

If you're not failing, you're not pushing your limits, and if you're not pushing your limits, you're not maximizing your potential.

Time is like a river that carries us forward into encounters with reality that require us to make decisions. We can't stop our movement down this river and we can't avoid those encounters. We can only approach them in the best possible way.

There are two broad approaches to decision making: evidence/logic-based (which comes from the higher-level brain) and subconscious/emotion-based (which comes from the lower-level animal brain).

Having the basics, a good bed to sleep in, good relationships, good food — is most important, and those things don't get much better when you have a lot of money or much worse when you have less. And the people one meets at the top aren't necessarily more special than those one meets at the bottom or in between.

Every game has principles that successful players master to achieve winning results. So does life.

Almost nothing can stop you from succeeding if you have flexibility and self-accountability.

Choose your habits well. Habit is probably the most powerful tool in your brain's toolbox.

By and large, life will give you what you deserve.

@RICHARD BRANSON

Business magnate, investor and founder of Virgin Group

The brave may not live forever, but the cautious do not live at all.

Do not be embarrassed by your failures, learn from them and start again.

My attitude has always been, if you fall flat on your face, at least you're moving forward. All you have to do is get back up and try again.

Too many people measure how successful they are by how much money they make or the people that they associate with. In my opinion, true success should be measured by how happy you are.

Business and awards don't mean that much. There is nothing more important than the health of you and your loved ones. Life is certainly too short not to appreciate people who have been significant in it.

I was dyslexic, I had no understanding of schoolwork whatsoever. I certainly would have failed IQ tests. And it was one of the reasons I left school when I was 15 years old. And if I'm not interested in something, I don't grasp it.

If somebody offers you an amazing opportunity but you are not sure you can do it, say yes and then learn how to do it later.

You don't learn to walk by following rules. You learn by doing, and by falling over.

Business opportunities are like buses, there's always another one coming.

@ROBERT IGER

Former CEO of Disney and author of The Ride Of A Lifetime

A little respect goes a long way, and the absence of it is often very costly.

What I've really learned over time is that optimism is a very, very important part of leadership.

If you approach and engage people with respect and empathy, the seemingly impossible can become real.

I think it is incredibly important to be open and accessible and treat people fairly and look them in the eye and tell them what is on your mind.

These are the ten principles that strike me as necessary to true leadership: Optimism, courage, focus, decisiveness, curiosity, fairness, thoughtfulness, authenticity, the relentless pursuit of perfection, and integrity.

People sometimes shy away from taking big swings because they assess the odds and build a case against trying something before they even take the first step.

It's not that I'm a daredevil. But I'm just generally not a fearful person. I don't conduct my life worrying about what could happen or what may happen.

Don't be in the business of playing it safe. Be in the business of creating possibilities for greatness.

Innovate or die, and there's no innovation if you operate out of fear of the new or untested.

The riskiest thing we can do is just maintain the status quo.

@ROBERT KIYOSAKI

Businessman and author of Rich Dad Poor Dad

You have to be smart. The easy days are over.

Face your fears and doubts, and new worlds will open to you.

Remember, your mind is your greatest asset, so be careful what you put into it.

If you want to go somewhere, it is best to find someone who has already been there.

Money is not the goal. Money has no value. The value comes from the dreams money helps achleve.

Academic qualifications are important and so is financial education. They're both important and schools are forgetting one of them.

The size of your success is measured by the strength of your desire; the size of your dream; and how you handle disappointment along the way.

A lot of people are afraid to tell the truth, to say no. That's where toughness comes into play. Toughness is not being a bully. It's having backbone.

The power of our thoughts may never be measured or appreciated, but it became obvious to me as a young boy that there was value and power in being aware of my thoughts and how I expressed myself.

The greatest story of all is Colonel Sanders. He didn't start until he was sixty-six on a freeway bypass for his chicken shop. Anything is possible!

If you've failed, that means you're doing something. If you're doing something, you have a chance.

The thing I always say to people is this: 'If you avoid failure, you also avoid success.'

When you are young, work to learn, not to earn.

Broke is temporary, poor is eternal.

@SAM WALTON

Entrepreneur and founder of Walmart

High expectations are the key to everything.

To succeed in this world, you have to change all the time.

Swim upstream. Go the other way. Ignore the conventional wisdom.

I have always been driven to buck the system, to innovate, to take things beyond where they've been.

If everybody is doing it one way, there's a good chance you can find your niche by going exactly in the opposite direction.

When somebody made a mistake — whether it was myself or anybody else — we talked about it, admitted it, tried to figure out how to correct it, and then moved on to the next day's work.

There is only one boss. The customer. And he can fire everybody in the company from the chairman on down, simply by spending his money somewhere else.

Nothing else can quite substitute for a few well-chosen, well-timed, sincere words of praise. They're absolutely free and worth a fortune.

It was almost as if I had a right to win. Thinking like that often seems to turn into sort of a self-fulfilling prophecy.

I had to pick myself up and get on with it, do it all over again, only even better this time.

You can make a positive out of the most negative if you work at it hard enough.

Loosen up, and everybody around you will loosen up.

You can learn from everybody.

@STEPHEN COVEY

Businessman, public speaker and author of The 7 Habits Of Highly Effective People

Start with the end in mind.

Life is not accumulation, it is about contribution.

Make time for planning; Wars are won in the general's tent.

There are three constants in life... change, choice and principles.

Your most important work is always ahead of you, never behind you.

The key is not to prioritize what's on your schedule, but to schedule your priorities.

If you carefully consider what you want to be said of you in the funeral experience, you will find your definition of success.

You have to decide what your highest priorities are and have the courage — pleasantly, smiling, unapologetically — to say 'no' to other things. And the way to do that is by having a bigger 'yes' burning inside.

Sow a thought, reap an action; sow an action, reap a habit; sow a habit, reap a character; sow a character, reap a destiny.

Trust is the glue of life. It's the most essential ingredient in effective communication. It's the foundational principle that holds all relationships.

Our character is basically a composite of our habits. Because they are consistent, often unconscious patterns, they constantly, daily, express our character.

The proactive approach to a mistake is to acknowledge it instantly, correct and learn from it.

If we keep doing what we're doing, we're going to keep getting what we're getting.

You can't talk your way out of problems you behave yourself into.

What you do has greater impact than what you say.

@STEVE JOBS

Business magnate, investor and co-founder of Apple Computers

Creativity is just connecting things.

You have to be burning with an idea, or a problem, or a wrong that you want to right. If you're not passionate enough from the start, you'll never stick it out.

You can't connect the dots looking forward; you can only connect them looking backwards. So you have to trust that the dots will somehow connect in your future.

Simple can be harder than complex: You have to work hard to get your thinking clean to make it simple. But it's worth it in the end because once you get there, you can move mountains.

Your time is limited, so don't waste it living someone else's life. Don't be trapped by dogma — which is living with the results of other people's thinking. Don't let the noise of others' opinions drown out your own inner voice. And most important, have the courage to follow your heart and intuition.

If you haven't found it yet, keep looking. Don't settle. As with all matters of the heart, you'll know when you find it. And, like any great relationship, it just gets better and better as the years roll on.

Remembering that you are going to die is the best way I know to avoid the trap of thinking you have something to lose. You are already naked. There is no reason not to follow your heart.

Being the richest man in the cemetery doesn't matter to me. Going to bed at night saying we've done something wonderful, that's what matters to me.

My favorite things in life don't cost any money. It's really clear that the most precious resource we all have is time.

@T. HARV ECKER

Businessman, motivational speaker and author of Secrets of the Millionaire Mind

How you do anything is how you do everything.

20% of your activities produce 80% of your results.

You would worry a lot less about what people think of you if you realized how little they do.

Money is a result. Wealth is a result. Health is a result. Your weight is a result. We live in a world of cause and effect.

If you are willing to do only what's easy, life will be hard. But if you are willing to do what's hard, life will be easy.

You need to recognize that your entire life is in your head. It's the way you think. It's the software system for your life computer, and if you want to change your life, it will have to start with the way you think. Choose your thoughts carefully.

If you want to change the fruit, you have to change the roots. If you want to change the visible, you have to change the invisible first.

For the rich, it's not about getting more stuff. It's about having the freedom to make almost any decision you want.

Never try to pull someone up who doesn't want it, they'll just pull you down.

Money will only make you more of what you already are.

Your income can only grow to the extent that you do.

Where attention goes, energy flows.

@THOMAS EDISON

Businessman and inventor of the first incandescent lightbulb

To have a great idea, have a lot of them.

Everything comes to him who hustles while he waits.

I have not failed. I've just found 10,000 ways that won't work.

When you have exhausted all possibilities, remember this: you haven't.

If we did all the things we are capable of, we would literally astound ourselves.

Our greatest weakness lies in giving up. The most certain way to succeed is always to try just one more time.

I know this world is ruled by infinite intelligence. Everything that surrounds us — everything that exists — proves that there are infinite laws behind it. There can be no denying this fact. It is mathematical in its precision.

Being busy does not always mean real work. The object of all work is production or accomplishment and to either of these ends there must be forethought, system, planning, intelligence, and honest purpose, as well as perspiration. Seeming to do is not doing.

Opportunity is missed by most people because it is dressed in overalls and looks like work.

Genius is one percent inspiration and ninety-nine percent perspiration.

Your worth consists in what you are and not in what you have.

What you are will show in what you do.

There is no substitute for hard work.

@TIMOTHY FERRISS

Entrepreneur, investor, podcaster and author of The 4-Hour Workweek

Lack of time is actually lack of priorities.

Focus on being productive instead of busy.

People will choose unhappiness over uncertainty.

What we fear doing most is usually what we most need to do.

An entrepreneur isn't someone who owns a business, it's someone who makes things happen.

Conditions are never perfect. 'Someday' is a disease that will take your dreams to the grave with you.

To enjoy life, you don't need fancy nonsense, but you do need to control your time and realize that most things just aren't as serious as you make them out to be.

99% of people in the world are convinced they are incapable of achieving great things, so they aim for the mediocre. The competition is thus fiercest for realistic goals.

You are the average of the five people you associate with most, so do not underestimate the effects of your pessimistic, unambitious, or disorganized friends. If someone isn't making you stronger, they're making you weaker.

If you are insecure, guess what? The rest of the world is, too. Do not overestimate the competition and underestimate yourself. You are better than you think.

The opposite of love is indifference, and the opposite of happiness is boredom.

Remember — boredom is the enemy, not some abstract failure.

If you let pride stop you, you will hate life.

Age doesn't matter: an open mind does.

@TONY HSIEH

Entrepreneur and venture capitalist

Chase the vision, not the money, the money will end up following you.

Have fun. The game is a lot more enjoyable when you're trying to do more than just make money.

Don't play the games that you don't understand, even if you see lots of other people making money from them.

The ultimate definition of success is: You could lose everything that you have and truly be okay with it. Your happiness isn't based on external factors.

I thought about how easily we are all brainwashed by our society and culture to stop thinking and just assume by default that more money equals more success and more happiness when ultimately happiness is really just about enjoying life.

Happiness is really just about four things: perceived control, perceived progress, connectedness (number and depth of your relationships), and vision/meaning (being part of something bigger than yourself).

There's a big difference between motivation and inspiration: Inspire through values and motivation takes care of itself.

In business you must do something that's above and beyond what's expected.

For individuals, character is destiny. For organizations, culture is destiny.

Learn by doing. Theory is nice but nothing replaces actual experience.

Without conscious effort, inertia always wins.

@TONY ROBBINS

Life coach, public speaker, philanthropist and author of Awaken the Giant Within

Your past does not equal your future.

The path to success is to take massive, determined action.

Identify your problems, but give your power and energy to solutions.

People are not lazy. They simply have impotent goals — that is, goals that do not inspire them.

A real decision is measured by the fact that you've taken a new action. If there's no action, you haven't truly decided.

I challenge you to make your life a masterpiece. I challenge you to join the ranks of those people who live what they teach, who walk their talk.

To effectively communicate, we must realize that we are all different in the way we perceive the world and use this understanding as a guide to our communication with others.

Quality questions create a quality life. Successful people ask better questions, and as a result, they get better answers.

Only those who have learned the power of sincere and selfless contribution experience life's deepest joy: true fulfillment.

It's not the events of our lives that shape us, but our beliefs as to what those events mean.

If you do what you've always done, you'll get what you've always gotten.

It's what you practice in private that you will be rewarded for in public.

@WALT DISNEY

Entrepreneur, animator, writer and film producer

It's kind of fun to do the impossible.

The way to get started is to quit talking and begin doing.

When you're curious, you find lots of interesting things to do.

All our dreams can come true, if we have the courage to pursue them.

When you believe in a thing, believe in it all the way, implicitly and unquestionable.

I always like to look on the optimistic side of life, but I am realistic enough to know that life is a complex matter.

All the adversity I've had in my life, all my troubles and obstacles, have strengthened me. You may not realize it when it happens, but a kick in the teeth may be the best thing in the world for you.

There is more treasure in books than in all the pirates' loot on Treasure Island and at the bottom of the Spanish Main and best of all, you can enjoy these riches every day of your life.

The more you like yourself, the less you are like anyone else, which makes you unique.

Why worry? If you've done the very best you can, worrying won't make it any better.

That's the real trouble with the world. Too many people grow up.

First, think. Second, believe. Third, dream. And finally, dare.

A person should never neglect their family for business.

@WARREN BUFFETT

Investor, philanthropist, chairman and CEO of Berkshire Hathaway

Risk comes from not knowing what you're doing.

Never invest in a business you cannot understand.

The most important investment you can make is in yourself.

If you don't find a way to make money while you sleep, you will work till you die.

Someone's sitting in the shade today because someone planted a tree a long time ago.

It takes 20 years to build a reputation and five minutes to ruin it. If you think about that, you'll do things differently.

No matter how great the talent or efforts, some things just take time. You can't produce a baby in one month by getting nine women pregnant.

It's better to hang out with people better than you. Pick out associates whose behavior is better than yours and you'll drift in that direction.

If you get to my age in life and nobody thinks well of you, I don't care how big your bank account is, your life is a disaster.

We simply attempt to be fearful when others are greedy and to be greedy only when others are fearful.

There seems to be some perverse human characteristic that likes to make easy things difficult.

The stock market is a device for transferring money from the impatient to the patient.

It's only when the tide goes out that you discover who's been swimming naked.

If you buy things you do not need, soon you will have to sell things you need.

Chains of habit are too light to be felt until they are too heavy to be broken.

@ZIG ZIGLAR

Salesman, motivational speaker and author of Embrace the Struggle

Your attitude, not your aptitude, will determine your altitude.

When you are tough on yourself, life is going to be infinitely easier on you.

Lack of direction, not lack of time, is the problem. We all have twenty-four hour days.

You don't have to be great at something to start, but you have to start to be great at something.

People often say that motivation doesn't last. Well, neither does bathing — that's why we recommend it daily.

Time can be an ally or an enemy. What it becomes depends entirely upon you, your goals, and your determination to use every available minute.

I believe that being successful means having a balance of success stories across the many areas of your life. You can't truly be considered successful in your business life if your home life is in shambles.

If you go out looking for friends, you're going to find they are very scarce. If you go out to be a friend, you'll find them everywhere.

What you get by achieving your goals is not as important as what you become by achieving your goals.

The chief cause of failure and unhappiness is trading what you want most for what you want right now.

Rich people have small TVs and big libraries, and poor people have small libraries and big TVs.

Expect the best. Prepare for the worst. Capitalize on what comes.

If you aim at nothing, you will hit it every time.

PART V

LEADERS

@ABRAHAM LINCOLN

Served as the 16th president of the United States from 1861 to 1865

All I have learned, I learned from books.

The best way to predict your future is to create it.

Folks are usually about as happy as they make their minds up to be.

That some achieve great success, is proof to all that others can achieve it as well.

Books serve to show a man that those original thoughts of his aren't very new at all.

A capacity, and taste, for reading gives access to whatever has already been discovered by others.

My great concern is not whether you have failed, but whether you are content with your failure.

We can complain because rose bushes have thorns, or rejoice because thorn bushes have roses.

Give me six hours to chop down a tree and I will spend the first four sharpening the axe.

Things may come to those who wait, but only the things left by those who hustle.

Discipline is choosing between what you want now and what you want most.

When I do good I feel good, when I do bad I feel bad, and that's my religion.

You cannot escape the responsibility of tomorrow by evading it today.

Those who look for the bad in people will surely find it.

Every person's happiness is their own responsibility.

Whatever you are, be a good one.

@ALEXANDER THE GREAT

King of the ancient Greek kingdom of Macedon

There is nothing impossible to him who will try.

With the right attitude, self-imposed limitations vanish.

I am indebted to my father for living, but to my teacher for living well.

Without knowledge, skill cannot be focused. Without skill, strength cannot be brought to bear and without strength, knowledge may not be applied.

As for a limit to one's labors, I, for one, do not recognize any for a high-minded man, except that the labors themselves should lead to noble accomplishments.

Through every generation of the human race there has been a constant war, a war with fear. Those who have the courage to conquer it are made free and those who are conquered by it are made to suffer until they have the courage to defeat it, or death takes them.

You shall, I question not, find a way to the top if you diligently seek for it; for nature hath placed nothing so high that is out of the reach of industry and valor.

Whatever possession we gain by our sword cannot be sure or lasting, but the love gained by kindness and moderation is certain and durable.

I am not afraid of an army of lions led by sheep; I am afraid of an army of sheep led by a lion.

Let us conduct ourselves so that all men wish to be our friends and all fear to be our enemies.

Remember, upon the conduct of each depends the fate of all.

In the end, when it's over, all that matters is what you've done.

@BENJAMIN FRANKLIN

A Founding Father of the United States

Lost time is never found again.

A penny saved is a penny earned.

By failing to prepare, you are preparing to fail.

Genius without education is like silver in the mine.

An investment in knowledge pays the best interest.

Life's tragedy is that we get old too soon and wise too late.

We are all born ignorant, but one must work hard to remain stupid.

Tell me and I forget. Teach me and I remember. Involve me and I learn.

Many people die at twenty-five and aren't buried until they are seventy-five.

There are three things extremely hard: steel, a diamond, and to know one's self.

There are two ways to increase your wealth. Increase your means or decrease your wants. The best is to do both at the same time.

Without continual growth and progress, such words as improvement, achievement, and success have no meaning.

Beware of little expenses. A small leak will sink a great ship.

Never leave that till tomorrow which you can do today.

An ounce of prevention is worth a pound of cure.

Whatever is begun in anger, ends in shame.

Well done is better than well said.

@DIANA FRANCES SPENCER

Princess of Wales

I'd like to be a queen in people's hearts.

When you are happy you can forgive a great deal.

I don't go by the rule book; I lead from the heart, not the head.

Anywhere I see suffering, that is where I want to be, doing what I can.

Helping people in need is a good and essential part of my life, a kind of destiny.

Every one of us needs to show how much we care for each other and, in the process, care for ourselves.

Carry out a random act of kindness, with no expectation of reward, safe in the knowledge that one day someone might do the same for you.

I think the biggest disease the world suffers from in this day and age is the disease of people feeling unloved. I know that I can give love for a minute, for half an hour, for a day, for a month, but I can give. I am very happy to do that, I want to do that.

They say it is better to be poor and happy than rich and miserable, but how about a compromise like moderately rich and just moody?

Everyone needs to be valued. Everyone has the potential to give something back.

You can't comfort the afflicted with afflicting the comfortable.

Family is the most important thing in the world.

@ELEANOR ROOSEVELT

First lady of the United States from 1933 to 1945

Do one thing every day that scares you.

It takes as much energy to wish as it does to plan.

A stumbling block to the pessimist is a stepping stone to the optimist.

Do what you feel in your heart to be right — for you will be criticized anyway.

Great minds discuss ideas; average minds discuss events; small minds discuss people.

You wouldn't worry so much about what others think of you if you realized how seldom they do.

Friendship with one's self is all important, because without it one cannot be friends with anyone else in the world.

Since you get more joy out of giving joy to others, you should put a good deal of thought into the happiness you are able to give.

You gain strength, courage, and confidence by every experience in which you really stop to look fear in the face. You are able to say to yourself, 'I lived through this horror. I can take the next thing that comes along.' You must do the thing you think you cannot do.

The purpose of life is to live it, to taste experience to the utmost, to reach out eagerly and without fear for newer and richer experience.

People grow through experience if they meet life honestly and courageously.

Tomorrow is a mystery. Today is a gift. That is why it is called the present.

No one can make you feel inferior without your consent.

It is better to light a candle than curse the darkness.

Happiness is not a goal; it is a by-product.

@ERNESTO CHE GUEVARA

Physician, author and guerrilla leader during the Cuban Revolution

Be realistic, demand the impossible.

Words that do not match deeds are unimportant.

Every day people straighten up their hair, why not their heart?

Above all, try to be able to feel deeply any injustice committed against any person in any part of the world.

The life of a single human being is worth a million times more than all the property of the richest man on earth.

Every person has the truth in his heart. No matter how complicated his circumstances, no matter how others look at him from the outside, and no matter how deep or shallow the truth dwells in his heart, once his heart is pierced with a crystal needle, the truth will gush forth like a geyser.

The world must not only be interpreted, it must be transformed. Man ceases to be the slave and tool of his environment and converts himself into the architect of his own destiny.

If you can find ways without any obstacles, it probably leads nowhere.

Live your life not celebrating victories, but overcoming defeats.

To accomplish much you must first lose everything.

Better to die standing than to live on your knees.

You can change the world.

@FREDERICK DOUGLASS

Social reformer, abolitionist, orator, writer and statesman

If there is no struggle, there can be no progress.

Freedom is a road seldom traveled by the multitude.

I didn't know I was a slave until I found out I couldn't do the things I wanted.

Some know the value of education by having it. I knew its value by not having it.

No man can put a chain about the ankle of his fellow man without at last finding the other end fastened about his own neck.

Those who profess to favor freedom, and yet deprecate agitation, are men who want crops without plowing up the ground. They want rain without thunder and lightning.

Where justice is denied, where poverty is enforced, where ignorance prevails, and where any one class is made to feel that society is an organized conspiracy to oppress, rob and degrade them, neither persons nor property will be safe.

I prefer to be true to myself, even at the hazard of incurring the ridicule of others, rather than to be false, and to incur my own abhorrence.

A man is worked upon by what he works on. He may carve out his circumstances, but his circumstances will carve him out as well.

People might not get all they work for in this world, but they must certainly work for all they get.

It is easier to build strong children than to repair broken men.

Once you learn to read, you will be forever free.

Knowledge makes a man unfit to be a slave.

@GAUTAMA BUDDHA

Religious leader who founded Buddhism

The mind is everything. What you think you become.

If you don't tend to one another, who then will tend to you?

Nothing can harm you as much as your own thoughts unguarded.

Three things cannot be long hidden: the sun, the moon, and the truth.

No one saves us but ourselves. No one can and no one may. We ourselves must walk the path.

Do not dwell in the past, do not dream of the future, concentrate the mind on the present moment.

Whatever words we utter should be chosen with care for people will hear them and be influenced by them for good or ill.

Holding on to anger is like grasping a hot coal with the intent of throwing it at someone else; you are the one who gets burned.

Thousands of candles can be lit from a single candle, and the life of the candle will not be shortened. Happiness never decreases by being shared.

If you knew what I know about the power of giving, you would not let a single meal pass without sharing it in some way.

Drop by drop is the water pot filled. Likewise, the wise man, gathering it little by little, fills himself with good.

To keep the body in good health is a duty, otherwise we shall not be able to keep our mind strong and clear.

Better than a thousand hollow words, is one word that brings peace.

People with opinions just go around bothering each other.

You only lose what you cling to.

@GEORGE WASHINGTON

Founding Father who served as the first president of the United States from 1789 to 1797

It is better to offer no excuse than a bad one.

Real men despise battle, but will never run from it.

Human happiness and moral duty are inseparably connected.

Be not glad at the misfortune of another, though he may be your enemy.

To be prepared for war is one of the most effective means of preserving peace.

Be courteous to all, but intimate with few, and let those few be well tried before you give them your confidence.

Associate yourself with men of good quality, if you esteem your own reputation; for 'tis better to be alone than in bad company.

True friendship is a plant of slow growth, and must undergo and withstand the shocks of adversity, before it is entitled to the appellation.

I hope I shall possess firmness and virtue enough to maintain what I consider the most enviable of all titles, the character of an honest man.

We should not look back unless it is to derive useful lessons from past errors, and for the purpose of profiting by dearly bought experience.

I conceive a knowledge of books is the basis upon which all other knowledge is to be built.

Perseverance and spirit have done wonders in all ages.

The harder the conflict, the greater the triumph.

@JACINDA ARDERN

40th Prime Minister of New Zealand

Everything I've ever thought about doing has been, in some sense, about helping people.

I want to be a good leader, not a good lady leader. I don't want to be known simply as the woman who gave birth.

The fact I'm the third female Prime Minister, I never grew up believing my gender would stand in the way of doing anything I wanted.

Lots of people juggle a lot of things in their personal and private lives, and I'm not unusual in that. Plenty of women have multitasked before me, and I want to acknowledge that.

I didn't think I would be prime minister, because I didn't consider it. But that's the power of saying yes, because there will be a moment when someone asks you to do something beyond your comfort zone. I am not unique.

One of the criticisms I've faced over the years is that I'm not aggressive enough or assertive enough, or maybe somehow, because I'm empathetic, it means I'm weak. I totally rebel against that. I refuse to believe that you cannot be both compassionate and strong.

The thing that drives people more often than not is they genuinely feel that they can make a difference. So that means there are nice people in politics.

If you sit and wait to feel like you are the most confident person in the room, you are probably going to be left by yourself.

You can't ask other people to believe you and vote for you if you don't back yourself.

@JESUS OF NAZARETH

Religious leader and central figure in Christianity

So I say to you, ask and it will be given to you; search, and you will find; knock, and the door will be opened for you.

Do not be anxious about tomorrow, for tomorrow will be anxious for itself. Let the day's own trouble be sufficient for the day.

If you bring forth what is within you, what you bring forth will save you. If you do not bring forth what is within you, what you do not bring forth will destroy you.

All the commandments: You shall not commit adultery, you shall not kill, you shall not steal, you shall not covet, and so on, are summed up in this single command: You must love your neighbor as yourself.

Give to everyone who begs from you; and of him who takes away your goods do not ask them again. And as you wish that men would do to you, do so to them.

Do to others whatever you would like them to do to you. This is the essence of all that is taught in the law of the prophets.

If you want to be perfect, go, sell your possessions and give to the poor, and you will have treasure in heaven.

For what shall it profit a man, if he gain the whole world, and suffer the loss of his soul?

@JOHN F. KENNEDY

Served as the 35th president of the United States from 1961 to 1963

If not us, who? If not now, when?

Those who dare to fail miserably can achieve greatly.

One person can make a difference, and everyone should try.

A man may die, nations may rise and fall, but an idea lives on.

The greater our knowledge increases the more our ignorance unfolds.

We must find time to stop and thank the people who make a difference in our lives.

As we express our gratitude, we must never forget that the highest appreciation is not to utter words, but to live by them.

The problems of the world cannot possibly be solved by skeptics or cynics whose horizons are limited by the obvious realities. We need men who can dream of things that never were and ask 'why not?'

Change is the law of life. And those who look only to the past or present are certain to miss the future.

There are risks and costs to action. But they are far less than the long-range risks of comfortable inaction.

Too often we enjoy the comfort of opinion without the discomfort of thought.

Mankind must put an end to war before war puts an end to mankind.

Efforts and courage are not enough without purpose and direction.

Conformity is the jailer of freedom and the enemy of growth.

Do not pray for easy lives. Pray to be stronger men.

The human mind is our fundamental resource.

@LHAMO THONDUP

14th Dalai Lama

The goal is not to be better than the other man, but your previous self.

Happiness is not something ready made. It comes from your own actions.

We can never obtain peace in the outer world until we make peace with ourselves.

Our prime purpose in this life is to help others. And if you can't help them, at least don't hurt them.

With realization of one's own potential and self-confidence in one's ability, one can build a better world.

People take different roads seeking fulfillment and happiness. Just because they're not on your road doesn't mean they've gotten lost.

Man sacrifices his health in order to make money. Then he sacrifices his money to recuperate his health. And then he is so anxious about the future that he does not enjoy the present; the result being that he does not live in the present or the future; he lives as if he is never going to die, and then dies having never really lived.

There is no need for temples, no need for complicated philosophies. My brain and my heart are my temples; my philosophy is kindness.

A disciplined mind leads to happiness, and an undisciplined mind leads to suffering.

If you think you are too small to make a difference, try sleeping with a mosquito.

Just one small positive thought in the morning can change your whole day.

@MAHATMA GANDHI

Leader of the campaign for India's independence from British rule

If you don't ask, you don't get it.

The future depends on what we do in the present.

It is health that is real wealth and not pieces of gold and silver.

The best way to find yourself is to lose yourself in the service of others.

Earth provides enough to satisfy every man's needs, but not every man's greed.

Strength doesn't come from physical capacity. It comes from an indomitable will.

Happiness is when what you think, what you say, and what you do are in harmony.

It's the action, not the fruit of the action, that's important. You have to do the right thing. It may not be in your power, may not be in your time, that there'll be any fruit. But that doesn't mean you stop doing the right thing. You may never know what results come from your action. But if you do nothing, there will be no result.

You must not lose faith in humanity. Humanity is like an ocean; if a few drops of the ocean are dirty, the ocean does not become dirty.

Though we may know Him by a thousand names, He is one and the same to us all.

First they ignore you, then they laugh at you, then they fight you, then you win.

Live as if you were to die tomorrow. Learn as if you were to live forever.

The weak can never forgive. Forgiveness is the attribute of the strong.

I will not let anyone walk through my mind with their dirty feet.

An eye for eye only ends up making the whole world blind.

Faith is not something to grasp, it is a state to grow into.

He is lost who is possessed by carnal desire.

@MALIK 'MALCOLM X' EL-SHABAZZ

Muslim minister and human rights activist

Truth is on the side of the oppressed.

Men who stand for nothing will fall for anything.

A wise man can play the part of a clown, but a clown can't play the part of a wise man.

Education is the passport to the future, for tomorrow belongs to those who prepare for it today.

Don't be in a hurry to condemn because he doesn't do what you do or think as you think or as fast. There was a time when you didn't know what you know today.

The media is the most powerful entity on earth. They have the power to make the innocent guilty and to make the guilty innocent, and that's power. Because they control the minds of the masses.

There is no better than adversity. Every defeat, every heartbreak, every loss, contains its own seed, its own lesson on how to improve your performance next time.

Children have a lesson adults should learn, to not be ashamed of failing, but to get up and try again.

All of our experiences fuse into our personality. Everything that ever happened to us is an ingredient.

We cannot think of being acceptable to others until we have first proven acceptable to ourselves.

If you have no critics you'll likely have no success.

Stumbling is not falling.

@MARGARET THATCHER

Prime Minister of the United Kingdom from 1979 to 1990

Pennies do not come from heaven. They have to be earned here on earth.

It is not the creation of wealth that is wrong, but the love of money for its own sake.

If you just set out to be liked, you will be prepared to compromise on anything at any time, and would achieve nothing.

Disciplining yourself to do what you know is right and important, although difficult, is the highroad to pride, self-esteem, and personal satisfaction.

Look at a day when you are supremely satisfied at the end. It's not a day when you lounge around doing nothing; it's a day you've had everything to do and you've done it.

What is success? I think it is a mixture of having a flair for the thing that you are doing; knowing that it is not enough, that you have got to have hard work and a certain sense of purpose.

I do not know anyone who has gotten to the top without hard work. That is the recipe. It will not always get you to the top, but it will get you pretty near.

People think that at the top there isn't much room. They tend to think of it as an Everest. My message is that there is tons of room at the top.

Being powerful is like being a lady. If you have to tell people you are, you aren't.

Don't follow the crowd, let the crowd follow you.

@MARTIN LUTHER KING JR.

Christian minister and leader of the civil rights movement

Seeing is not always believing.

The quality, not the longevity, of one's life is what is important.

Love is the only force capable of transforming an enemy into a friend.

Faith is taking the first step even when you don't see the whole staircase.

Darkness cannot drive out darkness; only light can do that. Hate cannot drive out hate; only love can do that.

If you can't fly, then run, if you can't run, then walk, if you can't walk, then crawl, but by all means keep moving.

Every man must decide whether he will walk in the light of creative altruism or in the darkness of destructive selfishness.

Be a bush if you can't be a tree. If you can't be a highway, just be a trail. If you can't be a sun, be a star. For it isn't by size that you win or fail. Be the best of whatever you are.

Those who are not looking for happiness are the most likely to find it, because those who are searching forget that the surest way to be happy is to seek happiness for others.

An individual has not started living until he can rise above the narrow confines of his individualistic concerns to the broader concerns of all humanity.

Life's most persistent and urgent question is, 'What are you doing for others?'

We must learn to live together as brothers or perish together as fools.

Wars are poor chisels for carving out peaceful tomorrows.

The time is always right to do what is right.

A riot is the language of the unheard.

@MOTHER MARY TERESA

Roman Catholic nun, missionary and a saint

Peace begins with a smile.

If you judge people, you have no time to love them.

Do not wait for leaders; do it alone, person to person.

We shall never know all the good that a simple smile can do.

It's not how much we give but how much love we put into giving.

Be faithful in small things because it is in them that your strength lies.

What can you do to promote world peace? Go home and love your family.

Kind words can be short and easy to speak, but their echoes are truly endless.

Let us always meet each other with a smile, for the smile is the beginning of love.

Spread love everywhere you go. Let no one ever come to you without leaving happier.

If you are humble nothing will touch you, neither praise nor disgrace, because you know what you are.

We need to find God, and he cannot be found in noise and restlessness. God is the friend of silence. See how nature — trees, flowers, grass — grows in silence; see the stars, the moon and the sun, how they move in silence. We need silence to be able to touch souls.

@NAPOLEON BONAPARTE

Military leader during the French Revolution

Imagination rules the world.

Ability is nothing without opportunity.

If you want a thing done well, do it yourself.

Courage is like love; it must have hope for nourishment.

Impossible is a word to be found only in the dictionary of fools.

Until you spread your wings, you'll have no idea how far you can fly.

Nothing is more difficult, and therefore more precious, than to be able to decide.

Take time to deliberate, but when the time for action has arrived, stop thinking and go.

Great ambition is the passion of a great character. Those endowed with it may perform very good or very bad acts. All depends on the principles which direct them.

The fool has one great advantage over a man of sense; he is always satisfied with himself.

You become strong by defying defeat and by turning loss and failure into success.

There are only two forces that unite men — fear and interest.

Never interrupt your enemy when he is making a mistake.

Victory belongs to the most persevering.

History is a set of lies agreed upon.

@NELSON MANDELA

Anti-apartheid revolutionary who served as President of South Africa from 1994 to 1999

Fools multiply when wise men are silent.

Resentment is like drinking poison and then hoping it will kill your enemies.

Education is the most powerful weapon which you can use to change the world.

One of the most difficult things is not to change society — but to change yourself.

To be free is not merely to cast off one's chains, but to live in a way that respects and enhances the freedom of others.

There is no passion to be found playing small — in settling for a life that is less than the one you are capable of living.

I learned that courage was not the absence of fear, but the triumph over it. The brave man is not he who does not feel afraid, but he who conquers that fear.

No one is born hating another person because of the color of his skin, or his background, or his religion. People must learn to hate, and if they can learn to hate, they can be taught to love, for love comes more naturally to the human heart than its opposite.

Everyone can rise above their circumstances and achieve success if they are dedicated to and passionate about what they do.

When people are determined they can overcome anything.

May your choices reflect your hopes, not your fears.

A winner is a dreamer who never gives up.

@PROPHET MUHAMMAD

Religious leader and the founder of Islam

Speak good or remain silent.

A kind word is a form of charity.

Remember your own faults when you want to mention it of others.

No two things have been combined better than knowledge and patience.

Those who are patient in adversity and forgive wrongs are the doers of excellence.

Happy is the man that avoids hardship, but how fine is the man that is afflicted and shows endurance.

What has reached you was never meant to miss you, and what has missed you was never meant to reach you.

Be kind, for whenever kindness becomes part of something, it beautifies it. Whenever it is taken from something, it leaves it tarnished.

Make things easy for people and not difficult. Give people good news and bring them joy, and do not turn them away.

The greatest jihad (struggle/striving) is to battle your own soul, to fight the evil within yourself.

None of you truly believes until he wishes for his brother what he wishes for himself.

Riches are not from an abundance of worldly good but from a contented mind.

Seek knowledge from cradle to the grave.

@ROSA PARKS

Activist in the civil rights movement

Each person must live their lives as a model for others.

You must never be fearful about what you are doing when it is right.

I would like to be remembered as a person who wanted to be free, so other people would be also free.

Stand for something or you will fall for anything. Today's mighty oak is yesterday's nut that held its ground.

I have learned over the years that when one's mind is made up, this diminishes fear; knowing what must be done does away with fear.

Whatever my individual desires were to be free, I was not alone. There were many others who felt the same way.

I believe we are here on the planet Earth to live, grow up and do what we can to make this world a better place for all people to enjoy freedom.

Memories of our lives, of our works and our deeds will continue in others.

@SIR EDMUND HILLARY

Mountaineer and first person to have climbed Mount Everest

Life's a bit like mountaineering — never look down.

Once I've decided to do something, I do usually try to carry it through to fruition.

People do not decide to become extraordinary. They decide to accomplish extraordinary things.

You don't have to be a fantastic hero to do certain things — to compete. You can be just an ordinary chap, sufficiently motivated to reach challenging goals.

I'm sure the feeling of fear, as long as you can take advantage of it and not be rendered useless by it, can make you extend yourself beyond what you would regard as your capacity. If you're afraid, the blood seems to flow freely through the veins, and you really do feel a sense of stimulation.

I am a lucky man. I have had a dream and it has come true, and that is not a thing that happens often to men.

I think it all comes down to motivation. If you really want to do something, you will work hard for it.

On the summit of Everest, I had a feeling of great satisfaction to be first there.

No one remembers who climbed Mount Everest the second time.

It is not the mountain we conquer but ourselves.

@SRI SRI RAVI SHANKAR

Spiritual leader

Recognize and honor your uniqueness.

Welcome each day with a genuine smile from within.

If you can win over your mind, you can win over the whole world.

Forgive yourself and forgive others; Don't chew on other's mistakes or your own mistakes.

Don't postpone your happiness until some perfect future date. Be happy now, tomorrow will take care of itself.

There is nothing to worry about. There will be tough times, nice times, good times and bad times. They all come in life and go. Nothing stays.

Every moment you spend on this planet, remember that you are here for a unique purpose and cause, far greater than to just eat, sleep, and talk.

Nothing in the world can bother you as much as your own mind, I tell you. In fact, others seem to be bothering you but it is not others, it is your own mind.

Yoga is not just doing some exercise, it is much more. It is to expand your awareness, sharpen your intellect and enhance your intuitive ability.

Turn your demand into gratefulness. The more grateful you are, more love comes your way.

If you want to make sense it has to come from silence.

Make your smile cheaper and anger expensive.

@THEODORE ROOSEVELT

Served as the 26th president of the United States from 1901 to 1909

Believe you can and you're halfway there.

Do what you can, with what you have, where you are.

Keep your eyes on the stars, and your feet on the ground.

It is hard to fail, but it is worse never to have tried to succeed.

I am only an average man but, by George, I work harder at it than the average man.

If you could kick the person in the pants responsible for most of your trouble, you wouldn't sit for a month.

In any moment of decision, the best thing you can do is the right thing, the next best thing is the wrong thing, and the worst thing you can do is nothing.

I don't pity any man who does hard work worth doing. I admire him. I pity the creature who does not work, at whichever end of the social scale he may regard himself as being.

It is only through labor and painful effort, by grim energy and resolute courage, that we move on to better things.

When you are asked if you can do a job, tell 'em, 'Certainly I can!' Then get busy and find out how to do it.

The most important single ingredient in the formula of success is knowing how to get along with people.

Great thoughts speak only to the thoughtful mind, but great actions speak to all mankind.

Courtesy is as much a mark of a gentleman as courage.

I am a part of everything that I have read.

@THOMAS JEFFERSON

Founding Father who served as the third president of the United States from 1801 to 1809

Honesty is the first chapter of the book of wisdom.

I believe that every human mind feels pleasure in doing good to another.

I'm a greater believer in luck, and I find the harder I work the more I have of it.

Do you want to know who you are? Don't ask. Act! Action will delineate and define you.

Nothing can stop the person with the right mental attitude from achieving their goal; nothing on earth can help the person with the wrong mental attitude.

It does me no injury for my neighbor to say there are twenty gods or no god. It neither picks my pocket nor breaks my leg.

To penetrate and dissipate these clouds of darkness, the general mind must be strengthened by education.

The man who reads nothing at all is better educated than the man who reads nothing but newspapers.

When angry, count to ten before you speak. If very angry, count to one hundred.

Do not bite at the bait of pleasure, till you know there is no hook beneath it.

Never spend your money before you have earned it.

@WINSTON CHURCHILL

Prime Minister of the United Kingdom from 1940 to 1945

The true guide of life is to do what is right.

To improve is to change, so to be perfect is to have changed often.

We make a living by what we get, but we make a life by what we give.

One always measures friendships by how they show up in bad weather.

I like things to happen, and if they don't happen I like to make them happen.

You will never get to the end of the journey if you stop to throw a stone at every dog that barks.

When you're 20 you care what everyone thinks, when you're 40 you stop caring what everyone thinks, when you're 60 you realize no one was thinking about you in the first place.

A pessimist sees the difficulty in every opportunity; an optimist sees the opportunity in every difficulty.

Courage is what it takes to stand up and speak. Courage is also what it takes to sit down and listen.

You have enemies? Good. That means you've stood up for something, sometime in your life.

For myself I am an optimist — it does not seem to be much use being anything else.

You must put your head into the lion's mouth if the performance is to be a success.

Success consists of going from failure to failure without loss of enthusiasm.

The empires of the future are the empires of the mind.

If you're going through hell, keep going.

PART VI

WRITERS

@AESOP

Fabulist and storyteller

Slow and steady wins the race.

Give assistance, not advice, in a crisis.

The gods help them that help themselves.

Never trust the advice of a man in difficulties.

After all is said and done, more is said than done.

Do not count your chickens before they are hatched.

A liar will not be believed, even when he speaks the truth.

We often give our enemies the means for our own destruction.

A crust eaten in peace is better than a banquet partaken in anxiety.

He that is discontented in one place will seldom be happy in another.

People often grudge others what they cannot enjoy themselves.

The unhappy derive comfort from the misfortunes of others.

It is thrifty to prepare today for the wants of tomorrow.

Outside show is a poor substitute for inner worth.

The smaller the mind the greater the conceit.

Self-conceit may lead to self destruction.

Gratitude is the sign of noble souls.

Familiarity breeds contempt.

@AMELIA EARHART

First female aviator to fly solo across the Atlantic Ocean and author

There's more to life than being a passenger.

Preparation, I have often said, is rightly two-thirds of any venture.

Decide whether or not the goal is worth the risks involved. If it is, stop worrying.

Everyone has oceans to fly, if they have the heart to do it. Is it reckless? Maybe. But what do dreams know of boundaries?

The most difficult thing is the decision to act, the rest is merely tenacity. The fears are paper tigers. You can do anything you decide to do. You can act to change and control your life; and the procedure, the process is its own reward.

A single act of kindness throws out roots in all directions, and the roots spring up and make new trees. The greatest work that kindness does to others is that it makes them kind themselves.

The more one does and sees and feels, the more one is able to do, and the more genuine may be one's appreciation of fundamental things like home, and love, and understanding companionship.

I believe that a girl should not do what she thinks she should do, but should find out through experience what she wants to do.

Never interrupt someone doing something you said couldn't be done.

Courage is the price that life exacts for granting peace.

The most effective way to do it, is to do it.

@ANNE FRANK

Holocaust victim who wrote The Diary Of A Young Girl

No one has ever become poor by giving.

In the long run, the sharpest weapon of all is a kind and gentle spirit.

Where there's hope, there's life. It fills us with fresh courage and makes us strong again.

I keep my ideals, because in spite of everything I still believe that people are really good at heart.

Human greatness does not lie in wealth or power, but in character and goodness. People are just people, and all people have faults and shortcomings, but all of us are born with a basic goodness.

Everyone has inside of him a piece of good news. The good news is that you don't know how great you can be! How much you can love! What you can accomplish! And what your potential is!

Parents can only give good advice or put them on the right paths, but the final forming of a person's character lies in their own hands.

As long as this exists, this sunshine and this cloudless sky, and as long as I can enjoy it, how can I be sad?

How wonderful it is that nobody need wait a single moment before starting to improve the world.

We all live with the objective of being happy; our lives are all different and yet the same.

Think of all the beauty still left around you and be happy.

Whoever is happy will make others happy too.

@BRIAN TRACY

Public speaker and author of Eat That Frog

Whatever you believe with feeling becomes your reality.

Today the greatest single source of wealth is between your ears.

It doesn't matter where you are coming from. All that matters is where you are going.

The key to success is to focus our conscious mind on things we desire not things we fear.

I've found that luck is quite predictable. If you want more luck, take more chances. Be more active. Show up more often.

Move out of your comfort zone. You can only grow if you are willing to feel awkward and uncomfortable when you try something new.

The more you seek security, the less of it you have. But the more you seek opportunity, the more likely it is that you will achieve the security that you desire.

If you raise your children to feel that they can accomplish any goal or task they decide upon, you will have succeeded as a parent and you will have given your children the greatest of all blessings.

Successful people are always looking for opportunities to help others. Unsuccessful people are always asking, 'What's in it for me?'

The more credit you give away, the more will come back to you. The more you help others, the more they will want to help you.

Decisiveness is a characteristic of high-performing men and women. Almost any decision is better than no decision at all.

Successful people are simply those with successful habits.

@CHARLES DICKENS

Author and social critic

We need never be ashamed of our tears.

There is a wisdom of the head, and there is a wisdom of the heart.

Every traveler has a home of his own, and he learns to appreciate it the more from his wandering.

I must be taken as I have been made. The success is not mine, the failure is not mine, but the two together make me.

Suffering has been stronger than all other teaching, and has taught me to understand what your heart used to be. I have been bent and broken, but I hope into a better shape.

My meaning simply is, that whatever I have tried to do in life, I have tried with all my heart to do well; that whatever I have devoted myself to I have devoted myself completely; that in great aims and in small, I have always been thoroughly in earnest.

Reflect upon your present blessings — of which every man has many — not on your past misfortunes, of which all men have some.

Family not only needs to consist of merely those whom we share blood, but also of those whom we'd give blood.

There is nothing in the world so irresistibly contagious as laughter and good humor.

Take nothing on its looks; take everything on evidence. There's no better rule.

No one is useless in this world who lightens the burdens of another.

@CHARLES DUHIGG

Author of The Power of Habit

The more you focus, the more that focus becomes a habit.

This is the real power of habit: the insight that your habits are what you choose them to be.

Habits, scientists say, emerge because the brain is constantly looking for ways to save effort.

When a habit emerges, the brain stops fully participating in decision making. It stops working so hard, or diverts focus to other tasks. So unless you deliberately fight a habit — unless you find new routines — the pattern will unfold automatically.

You can't suddenly say, 'I want a brand new habit tomorrow,' and expect it to be easy and effortless. At some point, if you're changing a really deep-seated behavior, you're going to have a moment of weakness.

Willpower isn't just a skill. It's a muscle, like the muscles in your arms or legs, and it gets tired as it works harder, so there's less power left over for other things.

As people strengthened their willpower muscles in one part of their lives — in the gym, or a money management program — that strength spilled over into what they ate or how hard they worked. Once willpower became stronger, it touched everything.

This is how willpower becomes a habit: by choosing a certain behavior ahead of time, and then following that routine when an inflection point arrives.

Change might not be fast and it isn't always easy. But with time and effort, almost any habit can be reshaped.

The Golden Rule of Habit Change: You can't extinguish a bad habit, you can only change it.

There's nothing you can't do if you get the habits right.

@DALE CARNEGIE

Author of How to Win Friends and Influence People

The only way to get the best of an argument is to avoid it.

A person who seeks all their applause from outside has their happiness in another's keeping.

Instead of worrying about what people say of you, why not spend time trying to accomplish something they will admire.

You can make more friends in two months by becoming genuinely interested in other people than you can in two years by trying to get other people interested in you.

When dealing with people, remember you are not dealing with creatures of logic, but creatures of emotion, creatures bristling with prejudices and motivated by pride and vanity.

Don't be afraid to give your best to what seemingly are small jobs. Every time you conquer one it makes you that much stronger. If you do the little jobs well, the big ones will tend to take care of themselves.

It isn't what you have, or who you are, or where you are, or what you are doing that makes you happy or unhappy. It is what you think about.

Most of the important things in the world have been accomplished by people who have kept on trying when there seemed to be no hope at all.

Develop success from failures. Discouragement and failure are two of the surest stepping stones to success.

If you want to conquer fear, don't sit home and think about it. Go out and get busy.

Success is getting what you want. Happiness is wanting what you get.

You never achieve success unless you like what you are doing.

@DARREN HARDY

Author of The Compound Effect

Your past doesn't define you, it prepares you.

Motivation without action, leads to self-delusion.

Doubt and fear steal more dreams than failure does.

Giving to others is the greatest gift you can give yourself.

You will never change your life until you change something you do daily. The secret of your success is found in your daily routine.

Everything you need to be great is already inside you. Stop waiting for someone or something to light your fire. YOU have the match.

When it comes to breaking old habits and starting new ones, remember to be patient with yourself. You've got to expect it's going to take time and effort before you see lasting results.

The dream in your heart may be bigger than the environment in which you find yourself. Sometimes you have to get out of that environment to see that dream fulfilled. It's like planting an oak sapling in a pot. Once it becomes rootbound, its growth is limited. It needs a great space to become a mighty oak. So do you.

Broke people talk about people and problems. Rich people talk about ideas and goals. Your conversation chooses your destiny.

Dreams come with strings attached: Hard work, determination, persistence, sacrifice, compromise, and passion.

When you define your goals, you give your brain something new to look for and focus on.

You can only control two things in your life: Your attitude and your actions.

In essence, you make your choices, and then your choices make you.

@DAVID J. SCHWARTZ

Author of The Magic of Thinking Big

The mind is what the mind is fed.

Success shuns the man who lacks ideas.

Think little goals and expect little achievements. Think big goals and win big success.

You will find that the more successful the individual, the less inclined they are to make excuses.

Most of us make two basic errors with respect to intelligence: 1. We underestimate our own brainpower. 2. We overestimate the other fellow's brainpower.

Believe it can be done. When you believe something can be done, really believe, your mind will find the ways to do it. Believing a solution paves the way to a solution.

Where success is concerned, people are not measured in inches, or pounds, or college degrees, or family background; they are measured by the size of their thinking. How big we think determines the size of our accomplishments.

A man big enough to be humble appears more confident than the insecure man who feels compelled to call attention to his accomplishments. A little modesty goes a long way.

All of us, more than we recognize, are products of the thinking around us. And much of this thinking is little, not big.

How we think shows through in how we act. Attitudes are mirrors of the mind. They reflect thinking.

To get others to do what you want them to do, you must see things through their eyes.

Hope is a start. But hope needs action to win victories.

Give your ideas value by acting on them.

@DEEPAK CHOPRA

Author of Perfect Health

Don't try to steer the river.

In the midst of movement and chaos, keep stillness inside of you.

No solution can ever be found by running in three different directions.

The most creative act you will ever undertake is the act of creating yourself.

Life gives you plenty of time to do whatever you want to do if you stay in the present moment.

If you focus on success, you'll have stress. But if you pursue excellence, success will be guaranteed.

Every time you are tempted to react in the same old way, ask if you want to be a prisoner of the past or a pioneer of the future.

Holding on to anything is like holding on to your breath. You will suffocate. The only way to get anything in the physical universe is by letting go of it. Let go and it will be yours forever.

I've worked all my life on the subject of awareness, whether it's awareness of the body, awareness of the mind, awareness of your emotions, awareness of your relationships, or awareness of your environment. I think the key to transforming your life is to be aware of who you are.

Ultimately spiritual awareness unfolds when you're flexible, when you're spontaneous, when you're detached, when you're easy on yourself and easy on others.

If you try to get rid of fear and anger without knowing their meaning, they will grow stronger and return.

Anything that is of value in life only multiplies when it is given.

@ECKHART TOLLE

Author of The Power of Now

To love is to recognize yourself in another.

Where there is anger, there is always pain underneath.

The more you live in the present moment, the more the fear of death disappears.

Sometimes letting things go is an act of far greater power than defending or hanging on.

People look to time in expectation that it will eventually make them happy, but you cannot find true happiness by looking toward the future.

Narrow your life down to this moment. Your life situation may be full of problems — most life situations are — but find out if you have a problem at this moment. Do you have a problem now?

Any action is often better than no action, especially if you have been stuck in an unhappy situation for a long time. If it is a mistake, at least you learn something, in which case it's no longer a mistake. If you remain stuck, you learn nothing.

Don't wait to be successful at some future point. Have a successful relationship with the present moment and be fully present in whatever you are doing. That is success.

Being spiritual has nothing to do with what you believe and everything to do with your state of consciousness.

Acknowledging the good that you already have in your life is the foundation for all abundance.

Words reduce reality to something the human mind can grasp, which isn't very much.

The primary cause of unhappiness is never the situation but your thoughts about it.

Rather than being your thoughts and emotions, be the awareness behind them.

Realize deeply that the present moment is all you ever have.

@ERIC 'GEORGE ORWELL' BLAIR

Novelist, essayist, journalist and author

Reality exists in the human mind, and nowhere else.

In a time of deceit telling the truth is a revolutionary act.

The best books are those that tell you what you know already.

People are only as good as their technical development allows them to be.

Men can only be happy when they do not assume that the object of life is happiness.

On the whole human beings want to be good, but not too good, and not quite all the time.

The choice for mankind lies between freedom and happiness and for the great bulk of mankind, happiness is better.

Doublethink means the power of holding two contradictory beliefs in one's mind simultaneously, and accepting both of them.

In general, the greater the understanding, the greater the delusion; the more intelligent, the less sane.

We may find in the long run that tinned food is a deadlier weapon than the machine-gun.

Who controls the past controls the future. Who controls the present controls the past.

Whoever is winning at the moment will always seem to be invincible.

Happiness can exist only in acceptance.

@ERNEST HEMINGWAY

Journalist, novelist and short story writer

Never confuse movement with action.

The best way to find out if you can trust somebody is to trust them.

Now is no time to think of what you do not have. Think of what you can do with what there is.

There is nothing noble in being superior to your fellow man; true nobility is being superior to your former self.

So far, about morals, I know only that what is moral is what you feel good after and what is immoral is what you feel bad after.

The best people possess a feeling for beauty, the courage to take risks, the discipline to tell the truth, the capacity for sacrifice. Ironically, their virtues make them vulnerable; they are often wounded, sometimes destroyed.

Worry a little bit every day and in a lifetime you will lose a couple of years. If something is wrong, fix it if you can. But train yourself not to worry: Worry never fixes anything.

Every man's life ends the same way. It is only the details of how he lived and how he died that distinguish one man from another.

The world breaks everyone, and afterward, some are strong at the broken places.

When people talk, listen completely. Most people never listen.

There is no friend as loyal as a book.

@FYODOR DOSTOYEVSKY

Novelist, short story writer, essayist and journalist

It takes something more than intelligence to act intelligently.

Happiness does not lie in happiness, but in the achievement of it.

Man only likes to count his troubles; he doesn't calculate his happiness.

To go wrong in one's own way is better than to go right in someone else's.

The cleverest of all, in my opinion, is the man who calls himself a fool at least once a month.

Deprived of meaningful work, men and women lose their reason for existence; they go stark, raving mad.

A man who lies to himself, and believes his own lies becomes unable to recognize truth, either in himself or in anyone else, and he ends up losing respect for himself and for others. When he has no respect for anyone, he can no longer love, and, in order to divert himself, having no love in him, he yields to his impulses, indulges in the lowest forms of pleasure, and behaves in the end like an animal. And it all comes from lying — lying to others and to yourself.

Love the animals, love the plants, love everything. If you love everything, you will perceive the divine mystery in things. Once you perceive it, you will begin to comprehend it better every day. And you will come at last to love the whole world with an all-embracing love.

The mystery of human existence lies not in just staying alive, but in finding something to live for.

There is no subject so old that something new cannot be said about it.

What is hell? I maintain that it is the suffering of being unable to love.

To live without hope is to cease to live.

@GEORGE S. CLASON

Author of The Richest Man in Babylon

Wealth, like a tree, grows from a tiny seed.

Where the determination is, the way can be found.

Money is plentiful for those who understand the simple laws which govern its acquisition.

Will power is but the unflinching purpose to carry the task you set for yourself to fulfillment.

If I set for myself a task, be it so trifling, I shall see it through. How else shall I have confidence in myself to do important things?

Proper preparation is the key to our success. Our acts can be no wiser than our thoughts. Our thinking can be no wiser than our understanding.

Advice is one thing that is freely given away, but watch that you only take what is worth having. Seek advice from those who are competent through their own experience and success to give it.

He who spends more than he earns is sowing the winds of needless self indulgence from which he is sure to reap the whirlwinds of trouble and humiliation.

It is true that money cannot buy happiness but it does make it possible for you to enjoy the best that the world has to offer.

If you desire to help thy friend, do so in a way that will not bring thy friend's burdens upon thyself.

Luck has a peculiar habit of favoring those who do not depend on it.

It costs nothing to ask wise advice from a good friend.

Wealth that comes quickly, goeth the same way.

@HARPER LEE

Novelist and author of To Kill a Mockingbird

Many receive advice, only the wise profit from it.

People generally see what they look for, and hear what they listen for.

The one thing that doesn't abide by majority rule is a person's conscience.

Prejudice, a dirty word, and faith, a clean one, have something in common: they both begin where reason ends.

As sure as time, history is repeating itself, and as sure as man is man, history is the last place he'll look for his lessons.

Sometimes the Bible in the hand of one man is worse than a whiskey bottle in the hand of (another)... There are just some kind of men who — who're so busy worrying about the next world they've never learned to live in this one, and you can look down the street and see the results.

It's never an insult to be called what somebody thinks is a bad name. It just shows you how poor that person is, it doesn't hurt you.

Real courage is when you know you're licked before you begin, but you begin anyway and see it through no matter what.

You never really understand a person until you consider things from his point of view.

Until I feared I would lose it, I never loved to read. One does not love breathing.

Things are never as bad as they seem.

@HELEN KELLER

Author, political activist, and lecturer

What I am looking for is not out there, it is in me.

Alone we can do so little; together we can do so much.

Keep your face to the sunshine and you cannot see the shadows.

Although the world is full of suffering, it is also full of the overcoming of it.

We could never learn to be brave and patient, if there were only joy in the world.

Optimism is the faith that leads to achievement. Nothing can be done without hope and confidence.

Self-pity is our worst enemy and if we yield to it, we can never do anything wise in this world.

No pessimist ever discovered the secret of the stars, or sailed to an uncharted land, or opened a new doorway for the human spirit.

Character cannot be developed in ease and quiet. Only through experiences of trial and suffering can the soul be strengthened, vision cleared, ambition inspired and success achieved.

When one door of happiness closes, another opens; but often we look so long at the closed door that we do not see the one which has been opened for us.

People do not like to think. If one thinks, one must reach conclusions. Conclusions are not always pleasant.

Life is a succession of lessons which must be lived to be understood.

One can never consent to creep when one feels an impulse to soar.

No one has a right to consume happiness without producing it.

Life is either a daring adventure, or nothing.

@HENRY DAVID THOREAU

Essayist, poet and philosopher

Our life is frittered away by detail — simplify, simplify.

What is the use of a house if you haven't got a tolerable planet to put it on?

I would rather sit on a pumpkin, and have it all to myself, than be crowded on a velvet cushion.

If you have built castles in the air, your work need not be lost; that is where they should be. Now put the foundations under them.

The cost of a thing is the amount of what I will call life which is required to be exchanged for it, immediately or in the long run.

You must live in the present, launch yourself on every wave, find your eternity in each moment. Fools stand on their island of opportunities and look toward another land. There is no other land; there is no other life but this.

If one advances confidently in the direction of his dreams, and endeavors to live the life which he has imagined, he will meet with a success unexpected in common hours.

Live in each season as it passes; breathe the air, drink the drink, taste the fruit, and resign yourself to the influence of the earth.

Do not be too moral. You may cheat yourself out of much life. Aim above morality. Be not simply good, be good for something.

Books are the treasured wealth of the world and the fit inheritance of generations and nations.

If we will be quiet and ready enough, we shall find compensation in every disappointment.

It's not what you look at that matters, it's what you see.

Our truest life is when we are in dreams awake.

@JACK CANFIELD

Co-author of Chicken Soup for the Soul

Vague goals produce vague results.

I generally find that comparison is the fast track to unhappiness.

To change bad habits, we must study the habits of successful role models.

I believe that people make their own luck by great preparation and good strategy.

There are essentially two things that will make you wise, the books you read and the people you meet.

It's a universal principle that you get more of what you think about, talk about, and feel strongly about.

You must take personal responsibility. You cannot change circumstances, the seasons, or the wind, but you can change yourself.

If you are clear about your goals and take several steps in the right direction everyday, eventually you will succeed. So decide what it is you want, write it down, review it constantly, and each day do something that moves you toward those goals.

People who ask confidently get more than those who are hesitant and uncertain. When you've figured out what you want to ask for, do it with certainty, boldness and confidence.

Everything you want is out there waiting for you to ask. Everything you want also wants you. But you have to take action to get it.

Decide what you want, believe you can have it, believe you deserve it and believe it's possible for you.

Gratitude is the single most important ingredient to living a successful and fulfilled life.

Everything you want is on the other side of fear.

@JAMES ALLEN

Author of As a Man Thinketh

The dreamers are the saviors of the world.

Circumstances do not make the man, they reveal him.

A man is literally what he thinks, his character being the complete sum of all his thoughts.

You are today where your thoughts have brought you; you will be tomorrow where your thoughts take you.

Men are anxious to improve their circumstances, but are unwilling to improve them-selves; they therefore remain bound.

If your real desire is to be good, there is no need to wait for the money before you do it; you can do it now, this very moment, right where you are.

Dream lofty dreams, and as you dream, so you shall become. Your vision is the promise of what you shall one day be; your ideal is the prophecy of what you shall at last unveil.

The man who does not shrink from self-crucifixion can never fail to accomplish the object upon which the heart is set.

He who would accomplish little must sacrifice little; he who would accomplish much must sacrifice much.

Above all be of single aim; have a legitimate and useful purpose, and devote yourself unreservedly to it.

They who have conquered doubt and fear have conquered failure.

No duty is more urgent than that of returning thanks.

@JAMES CLEAR

Author of Atomic Habits

Habits are the compound interest of self-improvement.

You do not rise to the level of your goals. You fall to the level of your systems.

Success is not a goal to reach or a finish line to cross. It is a system to improve, an endless process to refine.

Every action you take is a vote for the type of person you wish to become. No single instance will transform your beliefs, but as the votes build up, so does the evidence of your new identity.

All big things come from small beginnings. The seed of every habit is a single, tiny decision. But as that decision is repeated, a habit sprouts and grows stronger. Roots entrench themselves and branches grow. The task of breaking a bad habit is like uprooting a powerful oak within us. And the task of building a good habit is like cultivating a delicate flower one day at a time.

Success is never due to one thing, but failure can be. Sleeping well won't make you successful, but not sleeping enough will hold you back. Hard work is rarely enough without good strategy, but even the best strategy is useless without hard work. Many things are necessary, but not sufficient for success.

Reading is like a software update for your brain. Whenever you learn a new concept or idea, the "software" improves. You download new features and fix old bugs. In this way, reading a good book can give you a new way to view your life experiences. Your past is fixed, but your interpretation of it can change depending on the software you use to analyze it.

You know yourself mostly by your thoughts. Everyone else in the world knows you only by your actions. Remember this when you feel misunderstood. You have to do or say something for others to know how you feel.

You should be far more concerned with your current trajectory than with your current results.

@J.K. ROWLING

Author of the Harry Potter series

It matters not what someone is born, but what they grow to be.

Whatever money you might have, self-worth really lies in finding out what you do best.

I would like to be remembered as someone who did the best she could with the talent she had.

Happiness can be found, even in the darkest of times, if one only remembers to turn on the light.

Are you the sort of person who gloats when they see a woman fall, or the kind that celebrates a magnificent recovery?

I have never been remotely ashamed of having been depressed. Never. What's to be ashamed of? I went through a really rough time and I am quite proud that I got out of that.

Failure meant a stripping away of the inessential. I stopped pretending to myself that I was anything other than what I was, and began to direct all my energy into finishing the only work that mattered to me. Had I really succeeded at anything else, I might never have found the determination to succeed in the one arena I believed I truly belonged.

It is impossible to live without failing at something, unless you live so cautiously that you might as well not have lived at all, in which case you have failed by default.

We do not need magic to change the world, we carry all the power we need inside ourselves already: we have the power to imagine better.

You will never truly know yourself, or the strength of your relationships, until both have been tested by adversity.

Humans have a knack for choosing precisely the things that are worst for them.

It is our choices that show what we truly are, far more than our abilities.

@J.L. COLLINS

Author of The Simple Path to Wealth

Create the idea, you are never alone.

A magazine is simply a device to induce people to read advertising.

The lines between need and want are continually and intentionally blurred.

There are many things money can buy, but the most valuable of all is freedom.

Here are a few key guidelines to consider: Spend less than you earn, invest the surplus and avoid debt.

In the simplest terms: When you buy stock you are buying a part ownership in a company. When you buy bonds you are loaning money to a company or government agency.

'You know, if you could learn to cater to the king, you wouldn't have to live on rice and beans.' To which the monk replies: 'If you could learn to live on rice and beans, you wouldn't have to cater to the king.'

Most great leaders do not start as great leaders. They grow into great leaders. Will you do whatever it takes to scale your leadership as the demands of your enterprise grows?

In the end, it is impossible to have a great life unless it is a meaningful life. And it is very difficult to have a meaningful life without meaningful work.

Greatness is not a function of circumstance. Greatness, it turns out, is largely a matter of conscious choice and discipline.

The best students are those who never quite believe their professors.

Every responsibility you get, make it a pocket of greatness.

@JOHANN WOLFGANG VON GOETHE

Writer and statesman

Everything is hard before it is easy.

A person hears only what they understand.

Behavior is the mirror in which everyone shows their image.

Courage is the commitment to begin without any guarantee of success.

Knowing is not enough; we must apply. Willing is not enough; we must do.

Daring ideas are like chessmen moved forward. They may be beaten, but they may start a winning game.

To think is easy. To act is hard. But the hardest thing in the world is to act in accordance with your thinking.

Many people take no care of their money until they come nearly to the end of it, and others do the same with their time.

You can easily judge the character of a man by how he treats those who can do nothing for him.

Kindness is the golden chain by which society is bound together.

As soon as you trust yourself, you will know how to live.

The soul that sees beauty may sometimes walk alone.

Few people have the imagination for reality.

Nothing is worth more than this day.

@JOHN MILTON

Poet, historian and author of Paradise Lost

Luck is the residue of design.

He who destroys a good book kills reason itself.

Good, the more communicated, more abundant grows.

Long is the way and hard, that out of hell leads up to light.

To be blind is not miserable; not to be able to bear blindness, that is miserable.

He who reigns within himself and rules passions, desires, and fears is more than a king.

A mind is not to be changed by place or time. The mind is its own place, and in itself can make a heaven of hell or a hell of heaven.

Gratitude bestows reverence, allowing us to encounter everyday epiphanies, those transcendent moments of awe that change forever how we experience life and the world.

There is nothing that makes men rich and strong but that which they carry inside of them. True wealth is of the heart, not of the hand.

Innocence, once lost, can never be regained. Darkness, once gazed upon, can never be lost.

Never can true reconcilement grow where wounds of deadly hate have pierced so deep.

Who overcomes by force, hath overcome but half his foe.

Awake, arise or be forever fall'n.

@J.R.R. TOLKIEN

Author of The Hobbit and The Lord of the Rings

Short cuts make long delays.

Where there is life there is hope.

I will not say: do not weep; for not all tears are an evil.

Faithless is he that says farewell when the road darkens.

All that is gold does not glitter, not all those who wander are lost.

It is not the strength of the body that counts, but the strength of the spirit.

A man that flies from his fear may find that he has only taken a shortcut to meet it.

The wide world is all about you: you can fence yourselves in, but you cannot forever fence it out.

For myself, I find I become less cynical rather than more — remembering my own sins and follies; and realize that men's hearts are not often as bad as their acts, and very seldom as bad as their words.

If more of us valued food and cheer and song above hoarded gold, it would be a merrier world.

All we have to decide is what to do with the time that is given to us.

A box without hinges, key, or lid, yet golden treasure inside is hid.

It is useless to meet revenge with revenge; it will heal nothing.

You can only come to the morning through the shadows.

Moonlight drowns out all but the brightest stars.

Courage is found in unlikely places.

Little by little, one travels far.

@KAMAL RAVIKANT

Author of Love Yourself Like Your Life Depends on It

It's your mind. You can do whatever you want.

This I know: the mind, left to itself, repeats the same stories, the same loops. Mostly ones that don't serve us. So what's practical, what's transformative, is to consciously choose a thought.

If you had a thought once, it has no power over you. Repeat it again and again, especially with emotional intensity, feeling it, and over time, you're creating the grooves, the mental river. Then it controls you.

I once heard someone explain thoughts as this: we, as human beings, think that we're thinking. Not true. Most of the time, we're remembering. We're reliving memories. We're running familiar patterns and loops in our head. For happiness, for procrastination, for sadness. Fears, hopes, dreams, desires. We have loops for everything.

The key, at least for me, has been to let go. Let go of the ego, let go of attachments, let go of who I think I should be, who others think I should be. And as I do that, the real me emerges, far far better than the Kamal I projected to the world. There is a strength in this vulnerability that cannot be described, only experienced.

Instead of reading loads of self-help books, attending various seminars, listening to different preachers, we should just pick one thing. Something that feels true for us. Then practice it fiercely.

So I ask myself the question, "If I loved myself, truly and deeply, what would I do?" I love this question. There is no threat, no right or wrong answer, only an invitation to my truth in this present moment.

As you love yourself, life loves you back. I don't think it has a choice either. I can't explain how it works, but I know it to be true.

Real growth comes through intense, difficult, and challenging situations.

I can't erase the past, only learn from it.

@KRISTIN NEFF

Professor and author of Self Compassion

There's almost no one whom we treat as badly as ourselves.

If I have to feel better than you to feel good about myself, then how clearly am I really going to see you, or myself for that matter?

By giving ourselves unconditional kindness and comfort while embracing the human experience, difficult as it is, we avoid destructive patterns of fear, negativity, and isolation.

Compassion is, by definition, relational. Compassion literally means 'to suffer with', which implies a basic mutuality in the experience of suffering. The emotion of compassion springs from the recognition that the human experience is imperfect.

Being human is not about being any one particular way; it is about being as life creates you—with your own particular strengths and weaknesses, gifts and challenges, quirks and oddities.

Painful feelings are, by their very nature, temporary. They will weaken over time as long as we don't prolong or amplify them through resistance or avoidance. The only way to eventually free ourselves from debilitating pain, therefore, is to be with it as it is. The only way out is through.

Our successes and failures come and go—they neither define us nor do they determine our worthiness.

Remember that if you really want to motivate yourself, love is more powerful than fear.

The key to happiness was understanding that suffering is caused by resisting pain.

@LEO TOLSTOY

Novelist, short story writer, essayist and author

If you want to be happy, be.

True life is lived when tiny changes occur.

The strongest of all warriors are these two — Time and Patience.

Wrong does not cease to be wrong because the majority share in it.

Everyone thinks of changing the world, but no one thinks of changing themselves.

The only thing that we know is that we know nothing and that is the highest flight of human wisdom.

It's not given to people to judge what's right or wrong. People have eternally been mistaken and will be mistaken, and in nothing more than in what they consider right and wrong.

If one loves anyone, one loves the whole person, just as they are and not as one would like them to be.

Truth, like gold, is to be obtained not by its growth, but by washing away from it all that is not gold.

The most important knowledge is that which guides the way you lead your life.

There is no greatness where there is no simplicity, goodness and truth.

Respect was invented to cover the empty place where love should be.

Each person's task in life is to become an increasingly better person.

The sole meaning of life is to serve humanity.

@MALCOLM GLADWELL

Journalist and author of Outliers

Hard work is a prison sentence only if it does not have meaning.

We aren't, as human beings, very good at acting in our best interest.

It's very hard to find someone who's successful and dislikes what they do.

Outliers are those who have been given opportunities — and who have had the strength and presence of mind to seize them.

We have, as human beings, a storytelling problem. We're a bit too quick to come up with explanations for things we don't really have an explanation for.

The values of the world we inhabit and the people we surround ourselves with have a profound effect on who we are.

If you work hard enough and assert yourself, and use your mind and imagination, you can shape the world to your desires.

The key to good decision making is not knowledge. It is understanding. We are swimming in the former. We are desperately lacking in the latter.

Truly successful decision-making relies on a balance between deliberate and instinctive thinking.

There can be as much value in the blink of an eye as in months of rational analysis.

A lot of what is most beautiful about the world arises from struggle.

Achievement is talent plus preparation.

@MARK MANSON

Author of The Subtle Art of Not Giving a F@#k

Carefully choose what to care about.

Life is about not knowing and then doing something anyway.

To be happy we need something to solve. Happiness is therefore a form of action.

This is the most simple and basic component of life: our struggles determine our successes.

Life is essentially an endless series of problems. The solution to one problem is merely the creation of another.

If pursuing the positive is a negative, then pursuing the negative generates the positive. The pain you pursue in the gym results in better all-around health and energy. The failures in business are what lead to a better understanding of what's necessary to be successful.

Values underlie everything we are and do. If what we value is unhelpful, if what we consider success/failure is poorly chosen, then everything based upon those values — the thoughts, the emotions, the day-to-day feelings — will all be out of whack.

The desire for more positive experience is itself a negative experience. And, paradoxically, the acceptance of one's negative experience is itself a positive experience.

If you want to change how you see your problems, you have to change what you value and/or how you measure failure/success.

Being wrong opens us up to the possibility of change. Being wrong brings the opportunity for growth.

You can't build a better mind without challenging your own beliefs and assumptions.

The more something threatens your identity, the more you will avoid it.

@MARK VICTOR HANSEN

Co-author of Chicken Soup for the Soul

Don't think it, ink it.

In imagination, there's no limitation.

Focused mind power is one of the strongest forces on earth.

Money never starts an idea: it's the idea that starts the money.

Turn your troubles into treasures. Learn from them and grow from them.

Success is creating a state of mind that allows you to do whatever it is you really want.

When you know clearly what you want, you'll wake up every morning excited about life.

This is an absolute law: You've got to be rich inside to become and remain rich outside. Become rich inside and your mental equivalent will manifest in your experience.

You control your future, your destiny. What you think about comes about. By recording your dreams and goals on paper, you set in motion the process of becoming the person you most want to be. Put your future in good hands — your own.

Don't wait until everything is just right. There will always be challenges, obstacles and less than perfect conditions. So what. Get started now. With each step you take, you will grow stronger, more and more skilled, more and more self-confident and more and more successful.

Read books, listen to audios, and attend seminars, they are decades of wisdom reduced to invaluable hours.

When your self-worth goes up, your net worth goes up with it.

Whatever you're ready for is ready for you.

Big goals get big results.

@MAYA ANGELOU

Poet, memoirist and civil rights activist

Nothing will work unless you do.

I've learned that even when I have pains, I don't have to be one.

Success is liking yourself, liking what you do, and liking how you do it.

If you don't like something, change it. If you can't change it, change your attitude.

There is nothing so pitiful as a young cynic because he has gone from knowing nothing to believing nothing.

Most people don't grow up. It's too damn difficult. What happens is most people get older. That's the truth of it. They honor their credit cards, they find parking spaces, they marry, they have the nerve to have children, but they don't grow up.

I've learned that people will forget what you said, people will forget what you did, but people will never forget how you made them feel.

Seek patience and passion in equal amounts. Patience alone will not build the temple. Passion alone will destroy its walls.

You may not control all the events that happen to you, but you can decide not to be reduced by them.

Whatever you want to do, if you want to be great at it, you have to love it and be able to make sacrifices for it.

We delight in the beauty of the butterfly, but rarely admit the changes it has gone through to achieve that beauty.

If you're always trying to be normal you will never know how amazing you can be.

Hate, it has caused a lot of problems in the world, but has not solved one yet.

There is no greater agony than bearing an untold story inside you.

All great achievements require time.

@NAPOLEON HILL

Author of Think and Grow Rich

A goal is a dream with a deadline.

Action is the real measure of intelligence.

If you cannot do great things, do small things in a great way.

Whatever the mind of man can conceive and believe, it can achieve.

Weak desire brings weak results, just as a small fire makes a small amount of heat.

Desire is the starting point of all achievement, not a hope, not a wish, but a keen pulsating desire which transcends everything.

You are the master of your destiny. You can influence, direct and control your own environment. You can make your life what you want it to be.

Do not wait: the time will never be 'just right'. Start where you stand, and work whatever tools you may have at your command and better tools will be found as you go along.

Think twice before you speak, because your words and influence will plant the seed of either success or failure in the mind of another.

Every adversity, every failure, and every heartache, carries with it the seed of an equivalent or greater benefit.

Patience, persistence and perspiration make an unbeatable combination for success.

Strength and growth come only through continuous effort and struggle.

The way of success is the way of continuous pursuit of knowledge.

Our only limitations are those we set up in our own minds.

A quitter never wins and a winner never quits.

@NASSIM NICHOLAS TALEB

Essayist and author

Difficulty is what wakes up the genius.

Heroes are heroes because they are heroic in behavior, not because they won or lost.

A prophet is not someone with special visions, just someone blind to most of what others see.

People focus on role models; it is more effective to find anti models — people you don't want to resemble when you grow up.

A Stoic is someone who transforms fear into prudence, pain into transformation, mistakes into initiation, and desire into undertaking.

The psychologist Gerd Gigerenzer has a simple heuristic. Never ask the doctor what you should do. Ask him what he would do if he were in your place. You would be surprised at the difference.

They think that intelligence is about noticing things that are relevant (detecting patterns); in a complex world, intelligence consists in ignoring things that are irrelevant (avoiding false patterns).

Missing a train is only painful if you run after it! Likewise, not matching the idea of success others expect from you is only painful if that's what you are seeking.

What matters isn't what a person has or doesn't have; it is what he or she is afraid of losing.

The three most harmful addictions are heroin, carbohydrates, and a monthly salary.

Abundance is harder for us to handle than scarcity.

Things always become obvious after the fact.

@OLIVER WENDELL HOLMES SR.

Physician and poet

Have the courage to act instead of react.

Sin has many tools, but a lie is the handle which fits them all.

Speak clearly, if you speak at all; carve every word before you let it fall.

It's faith in something and enthusiasm for something that makes a life worth living.

Men do not quit playing because they grow old; they grow old because they quit playing.

The great thing in the world is not so much where we stand, as in what direction we are moving.

Many people die with their music still in them. Why is this so? Too often it is because they are always getting ready to live. Before they know it, time runs out.

To reach a port we must sail, sometimes with the wind, and sometimes against it. But we must not drift or lie at anchor.

Many ideas grow better when transplanted into another mind than in the one where they sprang up.

One's mind, once stretched by a new idea, never regains its original dimensions.

A moment's insight is sometimes worth a life's experience.

Love is the master key that opens the gates of happiness.

Truth, when not sought after, rarely comes to light.

The Amen of nature is always a flower.

@PAULO COELHO

Lyricist, novelist and author of The Alchemist

You are what you believe yourself to be.

Be brave. Take risks. Nothing can substitute experience.

You drown not by falling into a river, but by staying submerged in it.

It's the possibility of having a dream come true that makes life interesting.

Tell your heart that the fear of suffering is worse than the suffering itself. And no heart has ever suffered when it goes in search of its dream.

Accept what life offers you and try to drink from every cup. All wines should be tasted; some should only be sipped, but with others, drink the whole bottle.

When you find your path, you must not be afraid. You need to have sufficient courage to make mistakes. Disappointment, defeat, and despair are the tools God uses to show us the way.

Everyone seems to have a clear idea of how other people should lead their lives, but none about his or her own.

There is only one thing that makes a dream impossible to achieve: the fear of failure.

Don't waste your time with explanations: people only hear what they want to hear.

Remember that wherever your heart is, there you will find your treasure.

@RALPH WALDO EMERSON

Essayist, lecturer and philosopher

To be great is to be misunderstood.

Your actions speak so loudly, I cannot hear what you say.

Write it on your heart that every day is the best day in the year.

The invariable mark of wisdom is to see the miraculous in the common.

For every minute you remain angry, you give up sixty seconds of peace of mind.

You cannot do a kindness too soon, for you never know how soon it will be too late.

Do not go where the path may lead, go instead where there is no path and leave a trail.

Unless you try to do something beyond what you have already mastered, you will never grow.

To be yourself in a world that is constantly trying to make you something else is the greatest accomplishment.

Without ambition one starts nothing. Without work one finishes nothing. The prize will not be sent to you. You have to win it.

What lies behind us and what lies before us are tiny matters compared to what lies within us.

Shallow men believe in luck or in circumstance. Strong men believe in cause and effect.

The only person you are destined to become is the person you decide to be.

Once you make a decision, the universe conspires to make it happen.

Beware what you set your heart upon. For it surely shall be yours.

@RHONDA BYRNE

Author of The Secret

Your mind is shaping the world around you.

There is always something to be grateful for.

You must focus on abundance to bring more abundance to you.

Life doesn't just happen to you; you receive everything in your life based on what you've given.

Instead of focusing on the world's problems, give your attention and energy to trust, love, abundance, education and peace.

It is impossible to bring more into your life if you are feeling ungrateful about what you have. Why? Because the thoughts and feelings you emit as you feel ungrateful are all negative emotions.

You might think, 'I've got time to follow my dreams.' You don't have time. Life is short. The current life expectancy is 24,869 days. While some of us will live more days and some fewer, either way you have only a precious number of days to live this life, and so you do not have time to put off your dreams. It is now or never. If you don't do it now, you will keep putting it off, and you'll never do it. The time is now!

People go through their whole lives chasing everything in the material world, and they fail to discover the greatest treasure of all, which is within them.

Learn from your mistakes, otherwise you will have unnecessary pain.

Remember that your thoughts are the primary cause of everything.

Your imagination is an extremely powerful tool.

Everyone has the power to visualise.

@ROBERT COLLIER

Author of Riches Within Your Reach

All riches have their origin in mind. Wealth is in ideas — not money.

The first principle of success is desire — knowing what you want. Desire is the planting of your seed.

One might as well try to ride two horses moving in different directions, as to try to maintain in equal force two opposing or contradictory sets of desires.

Be sure to visualize only what you want. The law works both ways. If you visualize your worries and your fears, you will make them real. Control your thoughts and you will control circumstances. Conditions will be what you make them.

Our subconscious minds have no sense of humour, play no jokes and cannot tell the difference between reality and an imagined thought or image. What we continually think about eventually will manifest in our lives.

The great successful men of the world have used their imagination. They think ahead and create their mental picture in all its details, filling in here, adding a little there, altering this a bit and that a bit, but steadily building.

Any thought that is passed on to the subconscious often enough and convincingly enough is finally accepted.

Your chances of success in any undertaking can always be measured by your belief in yourself.

You have to sow before you can reap. You have to give before you can get.

Success is the sum of small efforts, repeated day in and day out.

If you don't make things happen then things will happen to you.

@ROBIN SHARMA

Author of The Monk Who Sold His Ferrari

Leadership is not a title, it's a behavior.

Your 'I CAN' is more important than your IQ.

Everything is created twice, first in the mind and then in reality.

Greatness comes by beginning something that doesn't end with you.

Fill your brain with giant dreams so that there's no space for petty pursuits.

To construct an awesome life, build your daily life around your deepest priorities.

Don't confuse activity with productivity. Many people are simply busy being busy.

The main reason we waste time on small things is that we haven't identified our big things.

Every thought plants a seed to one of your actions. Every action, good or bad, will yield a consequence. The person who takes good steps every day, cannot help but reap a harvest of awesome results.

Love is the secret weapon of the iconic entrepreneur. Work with love, lead with love, serve with love. Do these and you become undefeatable.

Every minute spent worrying about the way things were is a moment stolen from creating the way things can be.

To double your income and success, triple your investment in personal development and professional mastery.

What makes genius is not just the idea, but the execution around the idea to bring it to the world.

Ordinary people love entertainment. Extraordinary people adore education.

Give out what you most want to come back.

@RYAN HOLIDAY

Author of The Obstacle Is the Way

Life is hard, but we make it much harder.

Impressing people is utterly different from being truly impressive.

The news is notoriously inaccurate, and our memory of it is even worse.

First, see clearly. Next, act correctly. Finally, endure and accept the world as it is.

We are A to Z thinkers. Fretting about A, obsessing over Z, and yet forgetting all about B through Y.

Your potential, the absolute best you're capable of—that's the metric to measure yourself against.

Where the head goes, the body follows. Perception preceded action. Right action follows the right perspective.

We only have so much energy for our work, for our relationships, for ourselves. A smart person understands this and guards it carefully. Meanwhile, idiots focus on marginal productivity hacks and gains while they leak out energy each passing day.

As tough an idea as it often is to stomach, the best way to thrive in a world that requires grunt work is to stop seeing it as grunt work.

The obstacle in the path becomes the path. Never forget, within every obstacle is an opportunity to improve our condition.

When intelligent people read, they ask themselves a simple question: What do I plan to do with this information?

End of night thoughts: What bad habit did I curb today? How am I better? Were my actions just?

Genius often really is just persistence in disguise.

@SAMUEL 'MARK TWAIN' CLEMENS

Author, publisher and lecturer

The secret of getting ahead is getting started.

If you tell the truth, you don't have to remember anything.

Wrinkles should merely indicate where the smiles have been.

Kindness is the language which the deaf can hear and the blind can see.

Always do what is right. It will gratify half of mankind and astound the other.

When your friends begin to flatter you on how young you look, it's a sure sign you're getting old.

Keep away from people who try to belittle your ambitions. Small people always do that, but the really great make you feel that you, too, can become great.

Anger is an acid that can do more harm to the vessel in which it is stored than to anything on which it is poured.

Never argue with stupid people, they will drag you down to their level and then beat you with experience.

It is better to keep your mouth closed and let people think you are a fool than to open it and remove all doubt.

Don't go around saying the world owes you a living. The world owes you nothing. It was here first.

Never allow someone to be your priority while allowing yourself to be their option.

It's not the size of the dog in the fight, it's the size of the fight in the dog.

A person who won't read has no advantage over one who can't read.

Everything has its limit — iron ore cannot be educated into gold.

@SETH GODIN

Author of Purple Cow

Dig your well before you're thirsty.

If it scares you, it might be a good thing to try.

The cost of being wrong is less than the cost of doing nothing.

Being aware of your fear is smart. Overcoming it is the mark of a successful person.

Plans are great but missions are better. Missions survive when plans fail, and plans almost always fail.

If you are deliberately trying to create a future that feels safe, you will willfully ignore the future that is likely.

I think the most productive thing to do during times of change is to be your best self, not the best version of someone else.

Instead of wondering when your next vacation is, maybe you should set up a life you don't need to escape from.

The easiest thing is to react. The second easiest thing is to respond. But the hardest thing is to initiate.

We believe what we want to believe in, and once we believe something, it becomes a self-fulfilling truth.

The art of moving forward lies in understanding what to leave behind.

You're either remarkable or invisible. Make a choice.

If failure is not an option, then neither is success.

Liberate yourself from the need to be right.

@SØREN KIERKEGAARD

Theologian, poet, social critic and author

Once you label me you negate me.

Take away paradox from the thinker and you have a professor.

To dare is to lose one's footing momentarily. Not to dare is to lose oneself.

During the first period of a person's life the greatest danger is not to take the risk.

If anyone on the verge of action should judge himself according to the outcome, he would never begin.

Life is not a problem to be solved, but a reality to be experienced. It can only be understood backwards; but it must be lived forwards.

The Bible is very easy to understand. But we are a bunch of scheming swindlers. We pretend to be unable to understand it because we know very well that the minute we understand, we are obliged to act accordingly.

There are two ways to be fooled. One is to believe what isn't true; the other is to refuse to believe what is true.

The function of prayer is not to influence God, but rather to change the nature of the one who prays.

Most people pursue pleasure with such breathless haste that they hurry past it.

Patience is necessary, and one cannot reap immediately where one has sown.

Life has its own hidden forces which you can only discover by living.

Boredom is the root of all evil — the despairing refusal to be oneself.

Our life always expresses the result of our dominant thoughts.

@STAN LEE

Comic book writer and creative leader for Marvel Comics

You have to be appreciative.

With great power comes great responsibility.

I see myself in everything I write. All the good guys are me.

The only advice anybody can give is if you want to be a writer, keep writing. And read all you can, read everything.

Another definition of a hero is someone who is concerned about other people's well-being and will go out of his or her way to help them — even if there is no chance of a reward. That person who helps others simply because it should or must be done, and because it is the right thing to do, is indeed without a doubt, a real superhero.

I used to be embarrassed because I was just a comic book writer while other people were building bridges or going on to medical careers. And then I began to realize: entertainment is one of the most important things in people's lives. Without it they might go off the deep end. I feel that if you're able to entertain people, you're doing a good thing.

No one has a perfect life. Everybody has something that they wish was not the way it is.

I'm happiest when I'm working. If I'm not working, I feel like I'm wasting my time.

If you are interested in what you do, that keeps you going.

It's fun doing something that hasn't been done before.

Life is never completely without challenges.

I guess one person can make a difference.

@STEPHEN KING

Award winning author

Books are a uniquely portable magic.

Once I fell in love with books, I fell in love completely.

I had a period where I thought I might not be good enough to publish.

If you don't have the time to read, you don't have the time or the tools to write.

Every book you pick up has its own lesson or lessons, and quite often the bad books have more to teach than the good ones.

Books are the perfect entertainment: no commercials, no batteries, hours of enjoyment for each dollar spent. What I wonder is why everybody doesn't carry a book around for those inevitable dead spots in life.

Don't let the sun go down without saying thank you to someone, and without admitting to yourself that absolutely no one gets this far alone.

Talent is cheaper than table salt. What separates the talented individual from the successful one is a lot of hard work.

Monsters are real, and ghosts are real too. They live inside us, and sometimes, they win.

Life is like a wheel. Sooner or later, it always comes around to where you started again.

You cannot condemn a man for what may only be a figment of your own imagination.

There's no harm in hoping for the best as long as you're prepared for the worst.

The scariest moment is always just before you start.

Either get busy living or get busy dying.

Quiet people have the loudest minds.

@TOM PETERS

Author of In Search of Excellence

Test fast, fail fast, adjust fast.

If a window of opportunity appears, don't pull down the shade.

A passive approach to professional growth will leave you by the wayside.

The top athletes are consummate pros who work obsessively at their craft. Approach yours the same way.

You will be remembered, in the long haul, for the quality of your work, not the quantity of your work. No one evaluates Picasso based on the number of paintings he churned out.

Life is pretty simple: You do some stuff. Most fails. Some works. You do more of what works. If it works big, others quickly copy it. Then you do something else. The trick is the doing something else.

Regardless of age, regardless of position, regardless of the business we happen to be in, all of us need to understand the importance of branding. We are CEOs of our own companies: Me, Inc. To be in business today, our most important job is to be head marketer for the brand called You.

Mastery is great, but even that is not enough. You have to be able to change course without a bead of sweat, or remorse.

If I read a book that cost me $20 and I get one good idea, I've gotten one of the greatest bargains of all time.

Leaders don't create followers, they create more leaders.

Celebrate what you want to see more of.

@URSULA KROEBER LE GUIN

Author of The Left Hand of Darkness

To oppose something is to maintain it.

The only questions that really matter are the ones you ask yourself.

Nobody who says, 'I told you so' has ever been, or will ever be, a hero.

I believe that maturity is not an outgrowing, but a growing up: that an adult is not a dead child, but a child who survived.

I doubt that the imagination can be suppressed. If you truly eradicated it in a child, he would grow up to be an eggplant.

As great scientists have said and as all children know, it is above all by the imagination that we achieve perception, and compassion, and hope.

We read books to find out who we are. What other people, real or imaginary, do and think and feel... is an essential guide to our understanding of what we ourselves are and may become.

You can't crush ideas by suppressing them. You can only crush them by ignoring them. By refusing to think, refusing to change.

To learn which questions are unanswerable, and *not to answer them*: this skill is most needful in times of stress and darkness.

When action grows unprofitable, gather information; when information grows unprofitable, sleep.

It is good to have an end to journey toward, but it is the journey that matters in the end.

To light a candle is to cast a shadow.

@VICTOR HUGO

Poet, dramatist of the Romantic movement and novelist

Those who do not weep, do not see.

He who opens a school door, closes a prison.

Our mind is enriched by what we receive, our heart by what we give.

To learn to read is to light a fire; every syllable that is spelled out is a spark.

Where no plan is laid, where the disposal of time is surrendered merely to the chance of incidence, chaos will soon reign.

Teach the ignorant as much as you can; society is culpable in not providing a free education for all and it must answer for the night which it produces. If the soul is left in darkness, sins will be committed.

The future has several names. For the weak, it is impossible; for the fainthearted, it is unknown; but for the valiant, it is ideal.

Be as a bird perched on a frail branch that she feels bending beneath her, still she sings away all the same, knowing she has wings.

Change your opinions, keep to your principles; change your leaves, keep intact your roots.

Laughter is sunshine, it chases winter from the human face.

Even the darkest night will end and the sun will rise.

People do not lack strength; they lack will.

@WALLACE D. WATTLES

Author of The Science of Getting Rich

What I want for myself, I want for everybody.

The competitive mind is not the creative one.

There is never any hurry on the creative plane; and there is no lack of opportunity.

There are three motives for which we live; we live for the body, we live for the mind, we live for the soul.

To do things in a way you want to do them, you will have to acquire the ability to think the way you want to think; this is the first step toward getting rich.

The grateful mind is constantly fixated upon the best. Therefore it tends to become the best. It takes the form or character from the best, and will receive the best.

Guard your speech. Never speak of yourself, your affairs, or of anything else in a discouraged or discouraging way.

If you want to help the poor, demonstrate to them that they can become rich; prove it by getting rich yourself.

You are not mentally developed by what you read, but by what you think about what you read.

The very best thing you can do for the whole world is to make the most of yourself.

A thought is a substance, producing the thing that is imagined by the thought.

By thought, the thing you want is brought to you; by action you receive it.

No one ever got rich by studying poverty and thinking about poverty.

Do, every day, all that can be done that day.

PART VII

PHILOSOPHY

@ABU HAMID AL-GHAZALI

Philosopher and theologian

To get what you love, you must first be patient with what you hate.

Desire makes slaves out of kings, and patience makes kings out of slaves.

Knowledge without action is wastefulness and action without knowledge is foolishness.

We are creatures that love to blame the external, not realizing that the problem is usually internal.

All of a man's happiness is in his being the master of his ego, while all his suffering is in his ego being his master.

The way to Paradise is an uphill climb, whereas Hell is downhill. Hence, there is a struggle to Paradise and not to Hell.

What is destined will reach you, even if it be beneath two mountains. What is not destined will not reach you, even if it be between your two lips.

Live as long as you want, but you must die; love whatever you want, but you will become separated from it; and do what you want, but you will be repaid for it.

Four traits lift a person to the highest ranks, even if their works and knowledge are little: forbearance, humility, generosity, and good character. This is the perfection of faith.

Know that thankfulness is from the highest of stations, and it is higher than patience, fear, and detachment of the world.

The tongue is very small and light but it can take you to the greatest heights and it can put you in the lowest depths.

Take every effort to guard your tongue, as it is the strongest cause for your destruction.

@ALBERT EINSTEIN

Theoretical physicist

The true sign of intelligence is not knowledge but imagination.

Imagination is everything. It is the preview of life's coming attractions.

Few are those who see with their own eyes and feel with their own hearts.

Try not to become a man of success, but rather try to become a man of value.

I believe in intuitions and inspirations. I sometimes feel that I am right. I do not know that I am.

He who can no longer pause to wonder and stand rapt in awe, is as good as dead; his eyes are closed.

Learn from yesterday, live for today, hope for tomorrow. The important thing is not to stop questioning. Curiosity has its own reason for existing.

Only one who devotes himself to a cause with his whole strength and soul can be a true master. For this reason mastery demands all of a person.

Insanity: doing the same thing over and over again and expecting different results.

No problem can be solved from the same level of consciousness that created it.

Life is like riding a bicycle. To keep your balance you must keep moving.

If you can't explain it simply, you don't understand it well enough.

Unthinking respect for authority is the greatest enemy of truth.

In the middle of difficulty lies opportunity.

@ALBERT SCHWEITZER

Philosopher, physician, theologian, writer and humanitarian

The tragedy of life is what dies inside a man while he lives.

Think occasionally of the suffering of which you spare yourself the sight.

In the hopes of reaching the moon, we fail to see the flowers that blossom at our feet.

Success is not the key to happiness. Happiness is the key to success. If you love what you are doing, you will be successful.

Never say there is nothing beautiful in the world anymore. There is always something to make you wonder in the shape of a tree, the trembling of a leaf.

The thinking person must oppose all cruel customs, no matter how deeply rooted in tradition and surrounded by a halo. When we have a choice, we must avoid bringing torment and injury into the life of another.

You must not expect anything from others. It's you, of yourself, of whom you must ask a lot. Only from oneself has one the right to ask everything and anything. This way it's up to you — your own choices — what you get from others remains a present, a gift.

Constant kindness can accomplish much. As the sun makes ice melt, kindness causes misunderstanding, mistrust, and hostility to evaporate.

An optimist is a person who sees a green light everywhere, while a pessimist sees only the red spotlight, the truly wise person is colorblind.

The greatest thing is to give thanks for everything. He who has learned this knows what it means to live.

Do something for somebody every day for which you do not get paid.

@ARISTOTLE

Philosopher

Nature abhors a vacuum.

Happiness depends upon ourselves.

Those who know, do. Those that understand, teach.

No great mind has ever existed without a touch of madness.

We are what we repeatedly do. Excellence, then, is not an act, but a habit.

You will never do anything in this world without courage. It is the greatest quality of the mind next to honor.

I count him braver who overcomes his desires than him who conquers his enemies, for the hardest victory is over self.

Excellence is never an accident. It is always the result of high intention, sincere effort, and intelligent execution; it represents the wise choice of many alternatives — choice, not chance, determines your destiny.

One swallow does not make a summer, neither does one fine day; similarly one day or brief time of happiness does not make a person entirely happy.

It is the mark of an educated mind to be able to entertain a thought without accepting it.

Wishing to be friends is quick work, but friendship is a slow ripening fruit.

He who has overcome his fears will truly be free.

Patience is bitter, but its fruit is sweet.

A friend to all is a friend to none.

@ARTHUR SCHOPENHAUER

Philosopher and writer

Compassion is the basis of morality.

Will minus intellect constitutes vulgarity.

In action a great heart is the chief qualification. In work, a great head.

Almost all of our sorrows spring out of our relations with other people.

Every parting gives a foretaste of death, every reunion a hint of resurrection.

The more unintelligent a man is, the less mysterious existence seems to him.

Reading is equivalent to thinking with someone else's head instead of with one's own.

Religion is the masterpiece of the art of animal training, for it trains people as to how they shall think.

The wise have always said the same things, and fools, who are the majority have always done just the opposite.

All truth passes through three stages. First, it is ridiculed. Second, it is violently opposed. Third, it is accepted as being self-evident.

Money is human happiness in the abstract; he, then, who is no longer capable of enjoying human happiness in the concrete devotes himself utterly to money.

Wealth is like seawater; the more we drink, the thirstier we become; and the same is true of fame.

Wicked thoughts and worthless efforts gradually set their mark on the face, especially the eyes.

Every person takes the limits of their own field of vision for the limits of the world.

Talent hits a target no one else can hit; Genius hits a target no one else can see.

We forfeit three-quarters of ourselves in order to be like other people.

@BARUCH SPINOZA

Philosopher

All things excellent are as difficult as they are rare.

No matter how thin you slice it, there will always be two sides.

If you want the present to be different from the past, study the past.

Nothing in nature is random. A thing appears random only through the incompleteness of our knowledge.

The highest activity a human being can attain is learning for understanding, because to understand is to be free.

He who seeks to regulate everything by law is more likely to arouse vices than to reform them. It is best to grant what cannot be abolished, even though it be in itself harmful. How many evils spring from luxury, envy, avarice, drunkenness and the like, yet these are tolerated because they cannot be prevented by legal enactments.

The more you struggle to live, the less you live. Give up the notion that you must be sure of what you are doing. Instead, surrender to what is real within you, for that alone is sure....you are above everything distressing.

Happiness is not the reward of virtue, but is virtue itself; nor do we delight in happiness because we restrain from our lusts; but on the contrary, because we delight in it, therefore we are able to restrain them.

Those who know the true use of money, and regulate the measure of wealth according to their needs, live contented with few things.

When a man is prey to his emotions, he is not his own master.

I call him free who is led solely by reason.

@BLAISE PASCAL

Mathematician, physicist, inventor and writer

Imagination decides everything.

Nothing gives rest but the sincere search for truth.

Justice without force is powerless; force without justice is tyrannical.

Small minds are concerned with the extraordinary, great minds with the ordinary.

If we examine our thoughts, we shall find them always occupied with the past and the future.

Nature is an infinite sphere of which the center is everywhere and the circumference nowhere.

People are generally better persuaded by the reasons which they have themselves discovered than by those which have come into the mind of others.

Can anything be stupider than this: a man has the right to kill me because he lives on the other side of a river and his ruler has a quarrel with mine, though I have not quarrelled with him?

There are only two kinds of men: the righteous who think they are sinners and the sinners who think they are righteous.

The strength of a man's virtue should not be measured by his special exertions, but by his habitual acts.

If our condition were truly happy, we would not seek diversion from it in order to make ourselves happy.

All men's miseries derive from not being able to sit in a quiet room alone.

Do you wish people to think well of you? Don't speak well of yourself.

Kind words do not cost much. Yet they accomplish much.

Noble deeds that are concealed are most esteemed.

@CARL JUNG

Psychiatrist and psychoanalyst who founded analytical psychology

You are what you do, not what you say you'll do.

Thinking is difficult, that's why most people judge.

If one does not understand a person, one tends to regard him as a fool.

The shoe that fits one person pinches another; there is no recipe for living that suits all cases.

Every form of addiction is bad, no matter whether the narcotic be alcohol, morphine or idealism.

Your visions will become clear only when you can look into your own heart. Who looks outside, dreams; who looks inside, awakes.

Even a happy life cannot be without a measure of darkness, and the word 'happy' would lose its meaning if it were not balanced by sadness.

A human being would certainly not grow to be seventy or eighty years old if this longevity had no meaning for the species. The afternoon of human life must also have a significance of its own and cannot be merely a pitiful appendage to life's morning.

I shall not commit the fashionable stupidity of regarding everything I cannot explain as a fraud.

Knowing your own darkness is the best method for dealing with darknesses of other people.

Until you make the unconscious conscious, it will direct your life and you will call it fate.

I am not what happened to me, I am what I choose to become.

Knowledge rests not upon truth alone, but upon error also.

There is no coming to consciousness without pain.

@CARL R. ROGERS

Psychologist

We live by a perceptual 'map' which is never reality itself.

As no one else can know how we perceive, we are the best experts on ourselves.

Neither the Bible, nor the prophets, nor the revelations of God or of men... Nothing has priority over direct experience.

We cannot change, we cannot move away from what we are, until we thoroughly accept what we are. Then change seems to come about almost unnoticed.

Growth occurs when individuals confront problems, struggle to master them, and through that struggle develop new aspects of their skills, capacities, views about life.

People are just as wonderful as sunsets if you let them be. When I look at a sunset, I don't find myself saying, 'Soften the orange a bit on the right hand corner.' I don't try to control a sunset. I watch with awe as it unfolds.

A person is a fluid process, not a fixed and static entity; a flowing river of change, not a block of solid material; a continually changing constellation of potentialities, not a fixed quantity of traits.

We think we listen, but very rarely do we listen with real understanding, true empathy. Yet listening, of this very special kind, is one of the most potent forces for change that I know.

Being empathetic is seeing the world through the eyes of the other, not seeing your world reflected in their eyes.

A person cannot teach another person directly; a person can only facilitate another's learning.

The only person who is educated is the one who has learned how to learn and change.

@CAROL S. DWECK

Psychologist and author of Mindset: The New Psychology of Success

A growth mindset is the belief you can develop abilities.

Children love this idea that their brain is like a muscle that gets stronger as they use it.

No matter what your ability is, effort is what ignites that ability and turns it into accomplishment.

Most experts and great leaders agree that leaders are made, not born, and that they are made through their own drive for learning and self-improvement.

'Hard-working' is what gets the job done. You just see that year after year. The students who thrive are not necessarily the ones who come in with the perfect scores. It's the ones who love what they're doing and go at it vigorously.

When we praise children for their intelligence, we tell them that this is the name of the game: Look smart; don't risk making mistakes.

Test scores and measures of achievement tell you where a student is, but they don't tell you where a student could end up.

With a fixed mindset, you're so worried about how smart or talented you are, you don't take on challenges. You don't try new things.

Failure is information — we label it failure, but it's more like, 'This didn't work, I'm a problem solver, and I'll try something else.'

Picture your brain forming new connections as you meet the challenge and learn. Keep on going.

@CHARLES DARWIN

Naturalist, geologist and biologist

I am not apt to follow blindly the lead of other men.

It is always advisable to perceive clearly our ignorance.

The very essence of instinct is that it's followed independently of reason.

We stopped looking for monsters under our bed when we realized that they were inside us.

If the misery of the poor be caused not by the laws of nature, but by our institutions, great is our sin.

A monkey, after getting drunk on brandy, would never touch it again, and thus is much wiser than most men.

There is no fundamental difference between man and animals in their ability to feel pleasure and pain, happiness, and misery.

It is not the strongest of the species that survives, nor the most intelligent that survives. It is the one that is the most adaptable to change.

The highest possible stage in moral culture is when we recognize that we ought to control our thoughts.

Intelligence is based on how efficient a species became at doing the things they need to survive.

We are always slow in admitting any great change of which we do not see the intermediate steps.

False facts are highly injurious to the progress of science, for they often endure long.

A person who dares to waste one hour of time has not discovered the value of life.

The love for all living creatures is the most noble attribute of man.

A man's friendships are one of the best measures of his worth.

@CONFUCIOUS

Philosopher and politician

Wherever you go, go with all your heart.

You cannot open a book without learning something.

Real knowledge is to know the extent of one's ignorance.

Life is really simple, but we insist on making it complicated.

Before you embark on a journey of revenge, dig two graves.

It does not matter how slowly you go so long as you do not stop.

If you make a mistake and do not correct it, this is called a mistake.

Our greatest glory is not in never falling, but in rising every time we fall.

To see and listen to the wicked is already the beginning of wickedness.

Education breeds confidence. Confidence breeds hope. Hope breeds peace.

When it is obvious that the goals cannot be reached, don't adjust the goals, adjust the action steps.

The will to win, the desire to succeed, the urge to reach your full potential... these are the keys that will unlock the door to personal excellence.

If your plan is for one year, plant rice. If your plan is for 10 years plant trees. If your plan is for 100 years, educate children.

It is easy to hate and it is difficult to love. This is how the whole scheme of things works. All good things are difficult to achieve; and bad things are very easy to get.

We have two lives, and the second begins when realize we have one.

The man who moves a mountain begins by carrying away small stones.

A superior man is modest in his speech, but exceeds in his actions.

@ELISABETH KUBLER-ROSS

Psychiatrist and author

All events are blessings given to us to learn from.

Everything in this life has a purpose, there are no mistakes, no coincidences.

I believe that we are solely responsible for our choices, and we have to accept the consequences of every deed, word, and thought throughout our lifetime.

It's only when we truly know and understand that we have a limited time on earth — and that we have no way of knowing when our time is up — that we will begin to live each day to the fullest, as if it was the only one we had.

The most beautiful people we have known are those who have known defeat, known suffering, known struggle, known loss, and have found their way out of the depths. These persons have an appreciation, a sensitivity, and an understanding of life that fills them with compassion, gentleness, and a deep loving concern. Beautiful people do not just happen.

People are like stained-glass windows. They sparkle and shine when the sun is out, but when the darkness sets in, their true beauty is revealed only if there is a light from within.

There is no need to go to India or anywhere else to find peace. You will find that deep place of silence right in your room, your garden or even your bathtub.

The opinion which other people have of you is their problem, not yours.

Beauty gets the attention, personality gets the heart.

@EMILE COUE

Psychologist and pharmacist

Simplify always — do not complicate.

Always think that what you have to do is easy and it will become so.

It's not the number of years that makes you old, but the idea that you are getting old.

Nothing is impossible to us, except of course, that which is contrary to the laws of nature and the Universe.

Conscious auto-suggestion, made with confidence, faith, and perseverance realizes itself automatically, in all matters within reason.

We possess within us a force of incalculable power, which if we direct it in a conscious and wise manner, gives us the mastery of ourselves and allows us not only to escape from physical and mental ills, but also to live in relative happiness.

If you persuade yourself that you can do a certain thing, provided this thing be possible, you will do it, however difficult it may be. If, on the contrary, you imagine that you cannot do the simplest thing in the world, it is impossible for you to do it, and molehills become for you unscalable mountains.

The power of thought, of idea, is incommensurable, is immeasurable. The world is dominated by thought.

Every thought, good or bad, becomes concrete; it materializes and becomes a reality.

When you believe yourself to be a master of your thoughts, you become so.

Rich is he who thinks he is rich and poor is he who thinks he is poor.

@EPICTETUS

Stoic philosopher

Only the educated are free.

No man is free who is not master of himself.

If you want to improve, be content to be thought foolish and stupid.

It is impossible to begin to learn that which one thinks one already knows.

We have two ears and one mouth so that we can listen twice as much as we speak.

Whoever does not regard what he has as most ample wealth, is unhappy, though he be master of the world.

The essence of philosophy is that a man should so live that his happiness shall depend as little as possible on external things.

Be careful to leave your sons well instructed rather than rich, for the hopes of the instructed are better than the wealth of the ignorant.

Nothing great is created suddenly, any more than a bunch of grapes or a fig. If you tell me that you desire a fig, I answer you that there must be time. Let it first blossom, then bear fruit, then ripen.

Do not seek to bring things to pass in accordance with your wishes, but wish for them as they are, and you will find them.

Freedom is not procured by a full enjoyment of what is desired, but by controlling the desire.

People are not disturbed by things, but by the view they take of them.

Difficulties are things that show a person what they are.

Silence is safer than speech.

@FRIEDRICH NIETZSCHE

Philosopher, cultural critic, composer and poet

Without music, life would be a mistake.

That which does not kill us makes us stronger.

To live is to suffer, to survive is to find some meaning in the suffering.

The lonely one offers his hand too quickly to whomever he encounters.

It is not a lack of love, but a lack of friendship that makes unhappy marriages.

No one can construct for you the bridge upon which precisely you must cross the stream of life, no one but you yourself alone.

The surest way to corrupt a youth is to instruct him to hold in higher esteem those who think alike than those who think differently.

Today as always, men fall into two groups: slaves and free men. Whoever does not have two-thirds of his day for himself, is a slave, whatever he may be: a statesman, a businessman, an official, or a scholar.

The snake which cannot cast its skin has to die. As well the minds which are prevented from changing their opinions; they cease to be mind.

You have your way. I have my way. As for the right way, the correct way, and the only way, it does not exist.

Sometimes people don't want to hear the truth because they don't want their illusions destroyed.

To become what one is, one must not have the faintest idea what one is.

The higher we soar, the smaller we appear to those who cannot fly.

He whose life has a why can bear almost any how.

@GALILEO GALILEI

Astronomer, physicist and engineer

Knowing thyself, that is the greatest wisdom.

We cannot teach people anything; we can only help them discover it within themselves.

All truths are easy to understand once they are discovered; the point is to discover them.

There are those who reason well, but they are greatly outnumbered by those who reason badly.

To be humane, we must ever be ready to pronounce that wise, ingenious and modest statement 'I do not know'.

Nature is relentless and unchangeable, and it is indifferent as to whether its hidden reasons and actions are understandable to man or not.

Facts which at first seem improbable will, even on scant explanation, drop the cloak which has hidden them and stand forth in naked and simple beauty.

The deeper I go in considering the vanities of popular reasoning, the lighter and more foolish I find them. What greater stupidity can be imagined than that of calling jewels, silver, and gold 'precious,' and earth and soil 'base'?

I do not feel obliged to believe that the same God who has endowed us with senses, reason, and intellect has intended us to forego their use.

In the sciences, the authority of thousands of opinions is not worth as much as one tiny spark of reason in an individual man.

Who would set a limit to the mind of man? Who would dare assert that we know all there is to be known?

The bible shows the way to go to heaven, not the way the heavens go.

Where the senses fail us, reason must step in.

@HERACLITUS

Philosopher

Character is destiny.

All is flux, nothing stays still.

Much learning does not teach understanding.

If you do not expect the unexpected you will not find it, for it is not to be reached by search or trail.

To God everything is beautiful, good, and just; humans, however, think some things are unjust and others just.

Allow yourself to think only those thoughts that match your principles and can bear the bright light of day. Day by day, your choices, your thoughts, your actions fashion the person you become. Your integrity determines your destiny.

Good character is not formed in a week or a month. It is created little by little, day by day. Protracted and patient effort is needed to develop good character.

No man ever steps in the same river twice, for it's not the same river and he's not the same man.

The awake share a common world, but the asleep turn aside into private worlds.

Eyes and ears are poor witnesses to people if they have uncultured souls.

Our envy always lasts longer than the happiness of those we envy.

All things come into being by conflict of opposites.

There is nothing permanent except change.

@IMMANUEL KANT

Philosopher

Science is organized knowledge. Wisdom is organized life.

Thoughts without content are empty, intuitions without concepts are blind.

Space and time are the framework within which the mind is constrained to construct its experience of reality.

For peace to reign on Earth, humans must evolve into new beings who have learned to see the whole first.

He who is cruel to animals becomes hard also in his dealings with men. We can judge the heart of a man by his treatment of animals.

Without man and his potential for moral progress, the whole of reality would be a mere wilderness, a thing in vain, and have no final purpose.

Enlightenment is man's emergence from his self-imposed immaturity. Immaturity is the inability to use one's understanding without guidance from another.

Genius is the ability to independently arrive at and understand concepts that would normally have to be taught by another person.

How then is perfection to be sought? Wherein lies our hope? In education, and in nothing else.

The busier we are, the more acutely we feel that we live, the more conscious we are of life.

Experience without theory is blind, but theory without experience is mere intellectual play.

One who makes himself a worm cannot complain afterwards if people step on him.

We are not rich by what we possess but by what we can do without.

Ingratitude is the essence of vileness.

@JALAL AD-DIN MUHAMMAD RUMI BALKHI

Poet, theologian and scholar

What you seek is seeking you.

As you start to walk on the way, the way appears.

Why do you stay in prison when the door is so wide open?

Don't be satisfied with stories, how things have gone with others. Unfold your own myth.

It's your road, and yours alone, others may walk it with you, but no one can walk it for you.

Yesterday I was clever, so I wanted to change the world. Today I am wise, so I am changing myself.

Sell your cleverness and buy bewilderment. Cleverness is mere opinion. Bewilderment brings intuitive knowledge.

Your task is not to seek for love, but merely to seek and find all the barriers within yourself that you have built against it.

And so it is, that both the devil and the angelic spirits present us with objects of desire to awaken our power of choice.

Achieve some perfection yourself, so that you may not fall into sorrow by seeing the perfection in others.

Raise your words, not voice. It is rain that grows flowers, not thunder.

Don't grieve. Anything you lose comes round in another form.

Be empty of worrying. Think of who created thought.

Live life as if everything is rigged in your favor.

@JEAN-JACQUES ROUSSEAU

Philosopher, writer and composer

Rather suffer an injustice than commit one.

What wisdom can you find that is greater than kindness?

It is too difficult to think nobly when one thinks only of earning a living.

Conscience is the voice of the soul; the passions are the voice of the body.

We are reduced to asking others what we are. We never dare to ask ourselves.

Those that are most slow in making a promise are the most faithful in the performance of it.

Plants are shaped by cultivation and men by education. We are born weak, we need strength; we are born totally unprovided, we need aid; we are born stupid, we need judgment. Everything we do not have at our birth and which we need when we are grown is given to us by education.

Every man having been born free and master of himself, no one else may under any pretext whatever subject him without his consent. To assert that the son of a slave is born a slave is to assert that he is not born a man.

The money that we possess is the instrument of liberty, that which we lack and strive to obtain is the instrument of slavery.

What good would it be to possess the whole universe if one were its only survivor?

Insults are the arguments employed by those who are in the wrong.

No man has any natural authority over his fellow men.

Freedom is the power to choose our own chains.

Our greatest evils flow from ourselves.

@JOHN LOCKE

Philosopher and physician

What worries you, masters you.

No man's knowledge here can go beyond his experience.

I have always thought the actions of men the best interpreters of their thoughts.

Few men think, yet all will have opinions. Hence men's opinions are superficial and confused.

We are like chameleons. We take our hue and the color of our moral character, from those who are around us.

New opinions are always suspected, and usually opposed, without any other reason but because they are not common.

The great question which, in all ages, has disturbed mankind, and brought on them the greatest part of their mischiefs has been, not whether be power in the world, nor whence it came, but who should have it.

To love truth for truth's sake is the principal part of human perfection in this world, and the seed-plot of all other virtues.

Reading furnishes the mind only with materials of knowledge; it is thinking that makes what we read ours.

The only defense against the world is a thorough knowledge of it.

There are a thousand ways to wealth, but only one way to Heaven.

All wealth is the product of labor.

@JOHN MUIR

Environmental philosopher and author

The power of imagination makes us infinite.

Between every two pines is a doorway to a new world.

Everybody needs beauty as well as bread, places to play in and pray in, where nature may heal and give strength to body and soul.

Only by going alone in silence, without baggage, can one truly get into the heart of the wilderness. All other travel is mere dust and hotels and baggage and chatter.

From the dust of the earth, from the common elementary fund, the Creator has made Homo sapiens. From the same material he has made every other creature, however noxious and insignificant to us. They are earth-born companions and our fellow mortals.

Any fool can destroy trees. They cannot run away; and if they could, they would still be destroyed — chased and hunted down as long as fun or a dollar could be got out of their bark hides, branching horns, or magnificent bole backbones.

God has cared for these trees, saved them from drought, disease, avalanches, and a thousand tempests and floods. But he cannot save them from fools.

I only went out for a walk and finally concluded to stay out till sundown, for going out, I found, was really going in.

When one tugs at a single thing in nature, he finds it attached to the rest of the world.

The clearest way into the Universe is through a forest wilderness.

In every walk with nature one receives far more than he seeks.

@JORDAN PETERSON

Clinical psychologist, public speaker and author of 12 Rules for Life

When you have something to say, silence is a lie.

To suffer terribly and to know yourself as the cause: that is hell.

The successful among us delay gratification and bargain with the future.

Work as hard as you possibly can on at least one thing and see what happens.

The purpose of life is finding the largest burden that you can bear and bearing it.

Compare yourself with who you were yesterday, not to who someone else is today.

You don't get to choose not to pay a price, you only get to choose which price you pay.

The secret to your existence is right in front of you, and it manifests itself as all those things you know you should do but you're avoiding.

I don't tell people, 'You're okay the way that you are.' That's not the right story. The right story is, 'You're way less than you could be.'

Life is very difficult. One of the most ancient of religious ideas that emerges everywhere, I would say, is that life is essentially suffering.

It took untold generations to get you where you are. A little gratitude might be in order.

Perhaps you are overvaluing what you don't have and undervaluing what you do.

If you fulfill your obligations everyday you don't need to worry about the future.

Humility is recognition of personal insufficiency and the willingness to learn.

To learn is to die voluntarily and be born again, in great ways and small.

Love is the desire to see unnecessary suffering ameliorated.

@JULIUS CAESAR

Renowned general, politician and scholar

Experience is the teacher of all things.

Good reasons must, of course, give place to better.

Death, a necessary end, will come when it will come.

He conquers twice, who shows mercy to the conquered.

Men in general are quick to believe that which they wish to be true.

What we wish, we readily believe, and what we ourselves think, we imagine others think also.

Without training, they lacked knowledge. Without knowledge, they lacked confidence. Without confidence, they lacked victory.

Free yourself from the influence of hatred, friendship, anger, and pity: When these intervene, the mind cannot judge the truth, and no one ever served his emotions and his best interests simultaneously.

It is easier to find men who will volunteer to die, than to find those who are willing to endure pain with patience.

As a rule, men worry more about what they can't see than about what they can.

He has not learned the lesson of life who does not every day surmount a fear.

No one is so brave that he is not disturbed by something unexpected.

The greatest enemy will hide in the last place you would ever look.

Cowards die many times before their actual deaths.

We have not to fear anything, except fear itself.

@LAO TZU

Philosopher and writer

The heart that gives, gathers.

Silence is a source of great strength.

He who knows, does not speak. He who speaks, does not know.

A scholar who cherishes the love of comfort is not fit to be deemed a scholar.

The key to growth is the introduction of higher dimensions of consciousness into our awareness.

To realize that you do not understand is a virtue; Not to realize that you do not understand is a defect.

Do the difficult things while they are easy and do the great things while they are small. A journey of a thousand miles must begin with a single step.

Be content with what you have, rejoice in the way things are. When you realise there is nothing lacking, the whole world belongs to you.

Care about what other people think and you will always be their prisoner.

If you do not change direction, you may end up where you are heading.

Knowing others is wisdom, knowing yourself is enlightenment.

Nature does not hurry, yet everything is accomplished.

To a mind that is still, the whole universe surrenders.

By letting go, it all gets done.

@LEONARDO DA VINCI

Polymath whose areas of interest included drawing, painting, science and architecture

Wisdom is the daughter of experience.

The noblest pleasure is the joy of understanding.

One can have no smaller or greater mastery than mastery of oneself.

Learn how to see. Realize that everything connects to everything else.

Study without desire spoils the memory, and it retains nothing that it takes in.

Learning is the only thing the mind never exhausts, never fears, and never regrets.

One has no right to love or hate anything if one has not acquired a thorough knowledge of its nature.

There are three classes of people: those who see, those who see when they are shown, those who do not see.

Anyone who conducts an argument by appealing to authority is not using his intelligence; he is just using his memory.

Iron rusts from disuse; water loses its purity from stagnation ... even so does inaction sap the vigor of the mind.

As a well spent day brings happy sleep, so life well used brings happy death.

The greatest deception men suffer is from their own opinions.

Where the spirit does not work with the hand, there is no art.

He who wishes to be rich in a day will be hanged in a year.

Simplicity is the ultimate sophistication.

Nature never breaks her own laws.

@LUCIUS SENECA

Stoic philosopher

All cruelty springs from weakness.

We suffer more often in imagination than in reality.

Every new beginning comes from some other beginning's end.

Begin at once to live, and count each separate day as a separate life.

Wherever there is a human being, there is an opportunity for kindness.

It is not the man who has too little, but the man who craves more, that is poor.

The greatest blessings of mankind are within us and within our reach. A wise man is content with his lot, whatever it may be, without wishing for what he has not.

True happiness is to enjoy the present, without anxious dependence upon the future, not to amuse ourselves with either hopes or fears but to rest satisfied with what we have, which is sufficient, for he that is so, wants nothing.

It is not that we have so little time but that we lose so much. The life we receive is not short but we make it so; we are not ill provided but use what we have wastefully.

They lose the day in expectation of the night, and the night in fear of the dawn.

No person can have a peaceful life who thinks too much about lengthening it.

As is a tale, so is life: not how long it is, but how good it is, is what matters.

If a man knows not to which port he sails, no wind is favorable.

Associate with people who are likely to improve you.

Gratitude pays itself back in large measure.

Life, if well lived, is long enough.

@MARCUS AURELIUS

Stoic philosopher

What we do now echoes in eternity.

The soul becomes dyed with the color of its thoughts.

Don't be overheard complaining, not even to yourself.

If it is not right, do not do it, if it is not true, do not say it.

Waste no more time arguing what a good person should be. Be one.

Do every act of your life as though it were the very last act of your life.

It is not death that a man should fear, but he should fear never beginning to live.

Being attached to many things, we are weighed down and dragged along with them.

When you arise in the morning, think of what a precious privilege it is to be alive — to breathe, to think, to enjoy, to love.

Very little is needed to make a happy life; it is all within yourself, in your way of thinking.

You have power over your mind — not outside events. Realize this, and you will find strength.

It never ceases to amaze me: we all love ourselves more than other people, but care more about their opinions than our own.

Everything we hear is an opinion, not a fact. Everything we see is a perspective, not the truth.

How much more grievous are the consequences of anger than the causes of it.

Pleasures become punishments when taken beyond a certain point.

Learn to be indifferent to what makes no difference.

@MARCUS TULLIUS CICERO

Statesman, lawyer and philosopher

While there's life, there's hope.

No one can give you better advice than yourself.

A room without books is like a body without a soul.

If you have a garden and a library, you have everything you need.

Nature has planted in our minds an insatiable longing to see the truth.

To be ignorant of what occurred before you were born is to remain always a child.

It is the peculiar quality of a fool to perceive the faults of others and to forget his own.

The wise are instructed by reason, average minds by experience, the stupid by necessity and the brute by instinct.

If you pursue good with labour, the labour passes away but the good remains; if you pursue evil with pleasure, the pleasure passes away and the evil remains.

The art of life is to deal with problems as they arise, rather than destroy one's spirit by worrying about them too far in advance.

Do not hold the delusion that your advancement is accomplished by crushing others.

Gratitude is not only the greatest of virtues but the parent of all others.

Any man can make mistakes but only an idiot persists in his error.

The higher we are placed, the more humbly we should walk.

Silence is one of the great arts of conversation.

@MICHELANGELO

Sculptor, painter, poet and architect

Genius is eternal patience.

There's no greater harm than that of time wasted.

A man paints with his brain and not with his hands.

Our thoughts and imagination are the only real limits to our possibilities.

The idea is there locked inside. All you have to do is remove the excess stone.

There are no great limits to growth because there are no limits of human intelligence, imagination, and wonder.

Your gifts lie in the place where your values, passions and strengths meet. Discovering that place is the first step toward sculpting your masterpiece, your life.

The greatest danger for most of us is not that our aim is too high and we miss it, but that it is too low and we reach it.

If people knew how hard I worked to get my mastery, it wouldn't seem so wonderful at all.

However rich I may have been, I have always lived like a poor man.

Perfection is no small thing, but it is made up of small things.

No act of kindness, however small, is ever wasted.

Faith in oneself is the best and safest course.

@MIYAMOTO MUSASHI

Philosopher, swordsman, strategist and author of The Book of Five Rings

The Way is in training.

You can only fight the way you practice.

Perceive that which cannot be seen with the eye.

It may seem difficult at first, but everything is difficult at first.

Truth is not what you want it to be; it is what it is, and you must bend to its power or live a lie.

A man cannot understand the art he is studying if he only looks for the end result without taking the time to delve deeply into the reasoning of the study.

There is nothing outside of yourself that can ever enable you to get better, stronger, richer, quicker, or smarter. Everything is within. Everything exists. Seek nothing outside of yourself.

Perception is strong and sight weak. In strategy it is important to see distant things as if they were close and to take a distanced view of close things.

Control your anger. If you hold anger toward others, they have control over you. Your opponent can dominate and defeat you if you allow him to get you irritated.

Anyone can give up, it's the easiest thing in the world to do. But to hold it together when everyone else would understand if you fell apart, that's true strength.

You must understand that there is more than one path to the top of the mountain.

The approach to combat and everyday life should be the same.

If you wish to control others you must first control yourself.

Choose to live by choice, not by chance.

@NEIL DEGRASSE TYSON

Astrophysicist, cosmologist, planetary scientist and author

There is no greater education than one that is self driven.

Knowing how to think empowers you far beyond those who only know what to think.

No one is dumb who is curious. The people who don't ask questions remain clueless throughout their lives.

There's no shame in admitting what you don't know. The only shame is pretending you know all the answers.

We spend the first years of a child's life teaching it to walk and talk and the rest of its life to shut up and sit down. There's something wrong there.

For me, I am driven by two main philosophies: know more today about the world than I knew yesterday and lessen the suffering of others. You'd be surprised how far that gets you.

I said that if an alien came to visit, I'd be embarrassed to tell them that we fight wars to pull fossil fuels out of the ground to run our transportation. They'd be like, 'What?'

Even with all our technology and the inventions that make modern life so much easier than it once was, it takes just one big natural disaster to wipe all that away and remind us that, here on Earth, we're still at the mercy of nature.

We are all connected; To each other, biologically. To the earth, chemically. To the rest of the universe atomically.

The good thing about science is that it's true whether or not you believe in it.

@PABLO PICASSO

Painter, sculptor and theatre designer

Everything you can imagine is real.

The chief enemy of creativity is 'good' sense.

Inspiration does exist, but it must find you working.

What one does is what counts and not what one had the intention of doing.

Only put off until tomorrow what you are willing to die having left undone.

Others have seen what is and asked why. I have seen what could be and asked why not.

Our goals can only be reached through a vehicle of a plan, in which we must fervently believe, and upon which we must vigorously act. There is no other route to success.

Success is dangerous. One begins to copy oneself, and to copy oneself is more dangerous than to copy others. It leads to sterility.

He can who thinks he can, and he can't who thinks he can't. This is an inexorable, indisputable law.

Everything is a miracle. It is a miracle that one does not dissolve in one's bath like a lump of sugar.

I am always doing that which I cannot do, in order that I may learn how to do it.

The meaning of life is to find your gift. The purpose of life is to give it away.

To make oneself hated is more difficult than to make oneself loved.

Action is the foundational key to all success.

@PLATO

Philosopher

Courage is knowing what not to fear.

The beginning is the most important part of the work.

Never discourage anyone who continually makes progress, no matter how slow.

Human behavior flows from three main sources: desire, emotion, and knowledge.

Excellence is not a gift, but a skill that takes practice. We do not act 'rightly' because we are 'excellent', in fact we achieve 'excellence' by acting 'rightly'.

Apply yourself both now and in the next life. Without effort, you cannot be prosperous. Though the land be good, you cannot have an abundant crop without cultivation.

People are like dirt. They can either nourish you and help you grow as a person or they can stunt your growth and make you wilt and die.

We can easily forgive a child who is afraid of the dark; the real tragedy of life is when men are afraid of the light.

Wise men speak because they have something to say; Fools speak because they have to say something.

An empty vessel makes the loudest sound, so they that have the least wit are the greatest babblers.

False words are not only evil in themselves, but they infect the soul with evil.

Good actions give strength to ourselves and inspire good actions in others.

Be kind, for everyone you meet is fighting a hard battle.

Knowledge becomes evil if the aim be not virtuous.

The greatest wealth is to live content with little.

Beauty lies in the eyes of the beholder.

@PYTHAGORAS

Philosopher

Choices are the hinges of destiny.

No man is free who cannot control himself.

The art of living happily is to live in the present.

Wisdom thoroughly learned will never be forgotten.

Be silent or let thy words be worth more than silence.

A fool is known by his speech, and a wise man by silence.

Educate the children and it won't be necessary to punish the men.

As long as man continues to be the ruthless destroyer of lower living beings, he will never know health or peace.

If you have a wounded heart, touch it as little as you would an injured eye. There are only two remedies for the suffering of the soul: hope and patience.

The experience of life in a finite, limited body is specifically for the purpose of discovering and manifesting supernatural existence.

Friends are as companions on a journey, who ought to aid each other to persevere on the road to a happier life.

The oldest shortest words — yes and no are those which require the most thought.

Rest satisfied with doing well, and leave others to talk of you as they please.

Concern should drive us into action and not into depression.

Choose rather to be strong of soul than strong of body.

Above all things, respect yourself.

@RENE DESCARTES

Philosopher, mathematician and scientist

I think; therefore I am.

If you choose not to decide, you still have made a choice.

The thinking of the mind is twofold: understanding and willing.

We do not see the world we see, we see the world we can describe.

The reading of all good books is like a conversation with the finest minds of past centuries.

For the very fact that my knowledge is increasing little by little is the most certain argument for its imperfection.

If you would be a real seeker after truth, it is necessary that at least once in your life you doubt, as far as possible, all things.

Common sense is the most widely shared commodity in the world, for every man is convinced that he is well supplied with it.

It is not enough to have a good mind; the main thing is to use it well. It is not good enough to have good talent, the main thing is to apply it well.

Gratitude is a species of love, excited in us by some action of the person for whom we have it, and by which we believe that he has done some good to us, or at least that he has had the intention of doing so.

An optimist may see a light where there is none, but why must the pessimist always run to blow it out?

To know what people really think, pay regard to what they do, rather than what they say.

Control your body if you want your mind to work properly.

Conquer yourself rather than the world.

@ROBERT B. CIALDINI

Professor and author of Influence: The Psychology of Persuasion

The way to love anything is to realize that it might be lost.

Observers trying to decide what a man is like look closely at his actions.

Our best evidence of what people truly feel and believe comes less from their words than from their deeds.

We all fool ourselves from time to time in order to keep our thoughts and beliefs consistent with what we have already done or decided.

In general, when we are unsure of ourselves, when the situation is unclear or ambiguous, when uncertainty reigns, we are most likely to look to and accept the actions of others as correct.

A well-known principle of human behavior says that when we ask someone to do us a favor we will be more successful if we provide a reason. People simply like to have reasons for what they do.

The idea of potential loss plays a large role in human decision making. In fact, people seem to be more motivated by the thought of losing something than by the thought of gaining something of equal value.

Persons who go through a great deal of trouble or pain to attain something tend to value it more highly than persons who attain the same thing with a minimum of effort.

Our typical reaction to scarcity hinders our ability to think.

Embarrassment is a villain to be crushed.

@SALVADOR DALI

Surrealist artist

Have no fear of perfection — you'll never reach it.

Those who do not want to imitate anything, produce nothing.

A true artist is not one who is inspired, but one who inspires others.

Give me two hours a day of activity, and I'll take the other twenty-two in dreams.

It is not me who is the clown, but this monstrously cynical and so unconsciously naive society, which plays the game of seriousness in order better to hide its madness.

Mistakes are almost always of a sacred nature. Never try to correct them. On the contrary: rationalize them, understand them thoroughly. After that, it will be possible for you to sublimate them.

At the age of six I wanted to be a cook. At seven I wanted to be Napoleon. And my ambition has been growing steadily ever since.

There is only one difference between a madman and me. The madman thinks he is sane. I know I am mad.

The thermometer of success is merely the jealousy of the malcontents.

Intelligence without ambition is a bird without wings.

Everything alters me, but nothing changes me.

@SIGMUND FREUD

Neurologist and founder of psychoanalysis

Thought is action in rehearsal.

Maturity is the ability to postpone gratification.

Out of your vulnerabilities will come your strength.

Immorality, no less than morality, has at all times found support in religion.

Civilization began the first time an angry person cast a word instead of a rock.

One day, in retrospect, the years of struggle will strike you as the most beautiful.

Unexpressed emotions will never die. They are buried alive and will come forth later in uglier ways.

There is a powerful force within us, an unilluminated part of the mind — separate from the conscious mind that is constantly at work molding our thought, feelings, and actions.

Before you diagnose yourself with depression or low self-esteem, first make sure that you are not, in fact, just surrounded by unpleasant people.

If you don't like a person it's because they remind you of something you don't like about yourself.

I cannot think of any need in childhood as strong as the need for a father's protection.

The mind is like an iceberg, it floats with one-seventh of its bulk above water.

In the small matters trust the mind, in the large ones the heart.

Being entirely honest with oneself is a good exercise.

From error to error, one discovers the entire truth.

@SIR ISAAC NEWTON

Mathematician, physicist, astronomer, theologian and author

Genius is patience.

You have to make the rules, not follow them.

Truth is the offspring of silence and meditation.

No great discovery was ever made without a bold guess.

What we know is a drop, what we do not know is an ocean.

If others would think as hard as I did, then they would get similar results.

Truth is ever to be found in simplicity, and not in the multiplicity and confusion of things.

He who thinks half-heartedly will not believe in God; but he who really thinks has to believe in God.

If I have ever made any valuable discoveries, it has been due more to patient attention, than to any other talent.

Every body continues in its state of rest, or of uniform motion in a right line, unless it is compelled to change that state by forces impressed upon it.

If I have seen further than others, it is by standing upon the shoulders of giants.

Tact is the knack of making a point without making an enemy.

Live your life as an exclamation rather than an explanation.

We build too many walls and not enough bridges.

To every action there is always an equal reaction.

Nature is pleased with simplicity.

@SOCRATES

Philosopher

Wisdom begins in wonder.

An unexamined life is not worth living.

True knowledge exists in knowing that you know nothing.

Education is the kindling of a flame, not the filling of a vessel.

True wisdom comes to each of us when we realize how little we understand about life, ourselves, and the world around us.

Employ your time in improving yourself by other men's writings so that you shall come easily by what others have laboured for.

The secret of happiness, you see, is not found in seeking more, but in developing the capacity to enjoy less.

He who is not content with what he has, would not be content with what he would like to have.

Worthless people live only to eat and drink; people of worth eat and drink only to live.

When the debate is over, slander becomes the tool of the loser.

There is only one good, knowledge, and one evil, ignorance.

Contentment is natural wealth, luxury is artificial poverty.

Let him that would move the world first move himself.

I know nothing except the fact of my ignorance.

Beware the barrenness of a busy life.

To find yourself, think for yourself.

@STEPHEN HAWKING

Theoretical physicist, cosmologist and author

Life would be tragic if it weren't funny.

Intelligence is the ability to adapt to change.

If you understand the universe, you control it, in a way.

However difficult life may seem, there is always something you can do and succeed at.

I am just a child who has never grown up. I still keep asking these 'how' and 'why' questions. Occasionally, I find an answer.

Look up at the stars and not down at your feet. Try to make sense of what you see, and wonder about what makes the universe exist. Be curious.

I believe everyone should have a broad picture of how the universe operates and our place in it. It is a basic human desire. And it also puts our worries in perspective.

I have noticed even people who claim everything is predestined, and that we can do nothing to change it, look before they cross the road.

When one's expectations are reduced to zero, one really appreciates everything one does have.

The past, like the future, is indefinite and exists only as a spectrum of possibilities.

People won't have time for you if you are always angry or complaining.

Work gives you meaning and purpose and life is empty without it.

@SUN TZU

Philosopher, military strategist and author of The Art Of War

A leader leads by example not by force.

Opportunities multiply as they are seized.

Ponder and deliberate before you make a move.

One may know how to conquer without being able to do it.

The supreme art of war is to subdue the enemy without fighting.

In war, the way is to avoid what is strong, and strike at what is weak.

It is easy to love your friend, but sometimes the hardest lesson to learn is to love your enemy.

Victorious warriors win first and then go to war, while defeated warriors go to war first and then seek to win.

If you know the enemy and know yourself, you need not fear the result of a hundred battles. If you know yourself but not the enemy, for every victory gained you will also suffer a defeat. If you know neither the enemy nor yourself, you will succumb in every battle.

What the ancients called a clever fighter is one who not only wins, but excels in winning with ease.

If the mind is willing, the flesh could go on and on without many things.

Even the finest sword plunged into salt water will eventually rust.

To know your enemy, you must become your enemy.

In the midst of chaos, there is also opportunity.

The wise warrior avoids the battle.

@VIKTOR FRANKL

Neurologist, psychiatrist, Holocaust survivor and author of Man's Search for Meaning

A human being is a deciding being.

Ever more people today have the means to live, but no meaning to live for.

When we are no longer able to change a situation — we are challenged to change ourselves.

Live as if you were living a second time, and as though you had acted wrongly the first time.

Happiness must happen, and the same holds for success: you have to let it happen by not caring about it.

Between stimulus and response there is a space. In that space is our power to choose our response. In our response lies our growth and our freedom.

Everything can be taken from a man but one thing: the last of human freedoms — to choose one's attitude in any given set of circumstances, to choose one's own way.

If there is a meaning in life at all, then there must be a meaning in suffering. Suffering is an ineradicable part of life, even as fate and death. Without suffering and death, human life cannot be complete.

There is nothing in the world, I venture to say, that would so effectively help one to survive even the worst conditions as the knowledge that there is a meaning in one's life.

When a person can't find a deep sense of meaning, they distract themselves with pleasure.

Faith is trust in ultimate meaning.

@VINCENT VAN GOGH

Post-impressionist painter

I dream my painting and I paint my dream.

The only time I feel alive is when I'm painting.

I have nature and art and poetry, and if that is not enough, what is enough?

Normality is a paved road. It's comfortable to walk but no flowers grow on it.

If you hear a voice within you say — You cannot paint — then by all means paint, and that voice will be silenced.

Love many things, for therein lies the true strength, and whosoever loves much performs much, and can accomplish much, and what is done in love is done well.

The fishermen know that the sea is dangerous and the storm terrible, but they have never found these dangers sufficient reason for remaining ashore.

If one is master of one thing and understands one thing well, one has at the same time, insight into and understanding of many things.

The beginning is perhaps more difficult than anything else but keep heart, it will turn out alright.

Great things are done by a series of small things brought together.

Success is sometimes the outcome of a whole string of failures.

What would life be if we had no courage to attempt anything?

One must work and dare if one really wants to live.

@WILLIAM JAMES

Philosopher and psychologist

Compared to what we ought to be, we are half awake.

To change one's life: Start immediately. Do it flamboyantly.

The great use of life is to spend it for something that will outlast it.

Action may not bring happiness but there is no happiness without action.

The greatest weapon against stress is our ability to choose one thought over another.

A great many people think they are thinking when they are merely rearranging their prejudices.

If you believe that feeling bad or worrying long enough will change a past or future event, then you are residing on another planet with a different reality system.

Whenever you're in conflict with someone, there is one factor that can make the difference between damaging your relationship and deepening it. That factor is attitude.

The greatest discovery of my generation is that a human being can alter his life by altering his attitudes.

Be not afraid of life. Believe that life is worth living, and your belief will help create the fact.

Most people never run far enough on their first wind to find out they've got a second.

The deepest principle in human nature is the craving to be appreciated.

We don't laugh because we're happy — we're happy because we laugh.

The art of being wise is the art of knowing what to overlook.

Act as if what you do makes a difference. It does.

@ZHUANG ZHOU

Philosopher

Happiness is the absence of the striving for happiness.

To be truly ignorant, be content with your own knowledge.

Great wisdom is generous; petty wisdom is contentious. Great speech is impassioned, small speech cantankerous.

Men honor what lies within the sphere of their knowledge, but do not realize how dependent they are on what lies beyond it.

You can't discuss the ocean with a well frog — he's limited by the space he lives in. You can't discuss ice with a summer insect — he's bound to a single season.

We cling to our own point of view, as though everything depended on it. Yet our opinions have no permanence; like autumn and winter, they gradually pass away.

All existing things are really one. We regard those that are beautiful and rare as valuable, and those that are ugly as foul and rotten. The foul and rotten may come to be transformed into what is rare and valuable, and the rare and valuable into what is foul and rotten.

The wise man knows that it is better to sit on the banks of a remote mountain stream than to be emperor of the whole world.

For the wise man looks into space and he knows there are no limited dimensions.

Those who realize their folly are not true fools.

ABOUT THE AUTHOR

R.W. Roth is an entrepreneur, martial artist, yoga practitioner and Brazilian Jiu Jitsu coach. He wrote *Mindset Mentors* to share some of the tools and wisdom that had helped him create a healthy mindset following many uncertain periods in his life. That experience convinced him that the guidance and inspiration distilled in these quotes from exceptional achievers can help anyone who is open to what they have to say.

Contact: Instagram @r.w.roth

Lightning Source UK Ltd.
Milton Keynes UK
UKHW031117250621
386146UK00007B/999